Wha

Sh

MW01716493

"Pete's stories are a gift to readers who love well-told tales. His characters, sometimes humorous, sometimes not, are so believable you feel you're living the adventure. Reading about their escapades is a delight and a memorable event."
Sharon Singleton - Winner, Escondido Library Short Story Contest 2019

"Pete Peterson is much in demand as a writers group facilitator, particularly for his meaningful critiques. He lives the writer's life—an example for us to emulate—and Pete is a master storyteller as this collection proves. He spins fun, entertaining tales with vivid language that feels like it came from the pen of Mark Twain. Treat yourself to one of his short stories tonight."
Woodrow Wilson – Author *The Champagne Taste/Beer Budget Cookbook* and *Out of This World Stories*

"Pete Peterson's stories take readers away from the everyday world and keep them there until they discover what happens next. With his mixture of great writing and thoughtful themes, readers will look at life differently when they reach the satisfying ending of each tale. I look forward to more of Pete's stories in the future."
Michele Ivy Davis - Author of the award-winning novel *Evangeline Brown and the Cadillac Motel*

Acclaim for Pete's Long-awaited Short Story Collection

"Pete Peterson's writing caught my attention many years ago and I look forward to reading his stories whenever something new comes along. His glimpses of humanity are genuine and affecting. He has shown me a side of life I never knew existed; I get carried along with the strength of his storytelling and characterizations. This well-tailored collection of his extraordinary stories of life as it was lived in days gone by is a revelation as usual. He's a marvel!"
Faith McCune - PAWSitive Change Coach

"I met Pete at a Read and Critique group during a tough time in my life. His ready acceptance of people, particularly me, led me to listen carefully when he read from a novel-in-progress about a young man gruesomely scarred by a house fire, who learns to play the banjo and ends up on the stage at the Grand Ole Opry. This story intrigued me then, perhaps more so today. I was introduced to a previously unknown and primarily rural world where raging floods destroy crops and disrupt families; where house fires burn down houses and burn up people; where desperate men fight back with the only tools they have—their fists and indomitable spirit. Pete's stories introduce memorable characters who often face large odds—sometimes they win, sometimes they lose, but always the reader is entertained, nay beguiled; heart strings are tugged and new insights on the human condition revealed. Reading his stories will change how you feel and think about people and the world."
Don Willick, Ph.D. Sc. Rel. - Dartmouth University
Director New Literature Studies

Acclaim for Pete's Long-awaited Short Story Collection

"Pete knows how to capture one's attention through his style of writing. He understands a character-real or fictional and spins the story around the character's iconic feature, attitude and/or accomplishments. His writings are highly entertaining and super engaging."
Elie Hanania – Ph. D. and Thought Leader

"Pete Peterson and I go way back to our meets at a local writers' critique group. With his mixture of great writing and Southern accent, he yanked us into his settings and plunked us down for a finger-lickin' feast so well done as to make us smack our lips for another serving. His characters took on flesh and blood with such reality you swear you've met them somewhere. He takes us to those faraway places with strange sounding names that keep calling us back."
R.M. Dell'Orfano - Writing Group facilitator - Regular contributor to *New Oxford Review's, Narthex Blog Essays.*

"Peterson is a terrific storyteller. Everything he writes comes with a hefty dose of heart."
Cherie Kephart - award-winning author of
A Few Minor Adjustments

CREDITS

"After Midnight" first appeared in *Stoneslide Collective* (May 2016), The Paper (March 2018), Rambler's Choice (July 2018); "Winner Take All" appeared in *Raven's Perch* (January 2018), *The Paper* (May 2018), *Tales of Ten Anthology* (il fennore publishing-May 2018); "Embers that Linger So" appeared in *Sowers* and *Harvesters* (April 2017); *–A Berry College Publication;* "Rules for Dying" was in *Deadly Writers Patrol Issue 15:* "An Old-fashioned Fourth" first appeared in *Dead Mule School of Southern Literature* (July 2015), *Wilson's Review of Southern Literature* (2017), *The Paper* (June 2018); "Bridges to Cross" *Back Country Review* (May 2019) *Tattletale* (August 2019; "The Food Thief" was a finalist in Faulkner Foudation's *"Words and Music"* Writers Competition (2018).

AFTER MIDNIGHT

SHORT STORY COLLECTION

R. L. "PETE" PETERSON

After Midnight
Short Story Collection
Pete Peterson

ISBN 978-1-7339547-0-6

Editing
Colleen J. Pallamary
colleenpallamary.com

Layout
Gerry Strong
downdogpressbooks.com

TABLE OF CONTENTS

Introduction hy Joe Sartor,
Associate Professor Art (Emeritus)
Morehouse State University
Morehouse, Ketucky

ACKNOWLEDGEMENTS

To Nancy Anne and Frick and Frac and MTP. Colleen for seeing the possibilities. For all those poor suckers in countless Read and Critique groups who suffered along as I tried to learn the basics. Perhaps someday, somehow that will happen.

IT'S THE WATER PERHAPS

I've had the pleasure of knowing at least one of the distinguished Richard "Pete" Petersons in this world - there seems to be quite a few. The one I've known since grade school is a writer living in the environs of San Diego. In fact, there may be more than one outstanding Pete Peterson in that fair city. In any case, the Pete I know grew up in the Show Me State, along with myself. There, through the 1940s and 50s at our respective one room schoolhouses, within a taxable distance of the City of Fulton, we learned to read, write, and practice good sportsmanship in the Kingdom of Callaway.

I first encountered Pete on a sunny afternoon during our fifth-grade year, when his Sunrise Raisins soft ball team pitted itself against my Central School Fryers. As I recall the event, Pete was like a young lieutenant: catching, hitting, running, and cheering his Raisins to undeniable victory. I distinctly recall feeling overwhelmed by his competitive spirit. A friendly spirit; gentlemanly but determined.

Our lives soon fast-forwarded into the 50s. We became good friends in high school, blessed with good teachers and wonderful classmates. Graduation Day rolled around without waiting for stragglers. In the twinkling, the Class of '57, departed the familiar hallowed halls of youth to gather grown up experiences, wisdoms, disappointments and perhaps, a rose bud or two, should time permit.

From our graduating class of 1957, Fulton High School produced a remarkable number of able Fine Arts practitioners. Charles "Chuck" Smith earned a doctoral degree in music and became a nationally noted university conductor of choral music. Bob

Robertson became nationally recognized as a sculptor of western art, comparable to the likes of Frederick Remington with a tinge more humor. David Holt, after earning a degree in Civil Engineering, served our country from the cockpit of a jet fighter, before segueing into the art of designing and producing artistic furniture. As for me, I waffled between vocal and visual interests, finally deciding on a career as a university professor specializing in studio art. Pete enlisted in Marine Corps two weeks after high school graduation and served at United States Embassies before becoming a successful corporate salesperson. His short story published in Seventeen Magazine while in Marine boot camp, earned him $35.00 and two hours of standing at attention yelling, "I'm Private Peterson, not Ernest Hemingway." Today his fiction and nonfiction frequents literary magazines and national publications.

I have heard it said that the good works of these men, and that of countless other Fulton progeny, may be attributable to its native source: water. I like to think this is plausible. Stinson Creek, also known as Town Creek, flows languidly but not too lazily below Hockaday Hill. Its water has long been recognized for better than average clothes washings, bathing's, baptisms, and even wart removal. Studies pending, it may yet be validated as a tonic from which outstanding young artists and writers spring.

You'll find elemental traces of Stinson Creek creativity in the lives of most Fultonians, long before the advent of bottled water from far-away places. My contention, however, is that an important aspect of our classmate's artistic ability was fueled by this sometimes quiet, sometimes turbulent tributary that meanders beneath the Second Street Bridge alongside the baseball park where Pete played many a game. This viewpoint gains credibility when one realizes Bob Robertson also fired his twisting curve balls and floating knuckler there. Smith, Holt and Sartor often watched from the stands, slaking our thirst at the water fountain. At the time, I'm sure I noticed certain warm vibrations on the right side of my brain, as I drank and always felt 100% hydration from this mystical source.

After one of Pete's games I've been told, his thirst quenched and mood heightened, he induced a group of school mates to climb to the top of Fulton's water tower – a tall and massive structure. Not just because it was there, but, well just to do it. This may also suggest these climbers enjoyed improved night vision and energy enhancement, good to the last drop, from the water ingested hours earlier. After midnight, but still freshly fueled.

Oh, how I'd like to hoist a big glass of Fulton's Town Creek water this very moment and toast the publication of Pete's short story collection, many set in the town of Volney, which I have a hunch is Fulton disguised. It will be a joy and satisfaction to hear his voice in print. Too long I've strained my eyesight in front of a laptop to partake of his interesting tales. Now I look forward to reading them in book form. I hope you join me.

Meanwhile, I thank my lucky stars to have drunk from the same well as Peterson, Robertson, Holt, and Smith, to have lived long enough to brag of Town Creek's mysterious powers. After reading Pete's book, I know I'm going to want to go back home for a transfusion of that elixir - be restored again - so I can keep on painting. That's how good stories and good pictures are created, by writing and painting and re-writing and re-painting until the essence emerge and then tomorrow paint and write and rewrite and repaint, again. That's why water is so important. It fuels the soul.

Joe Sartor
Associate Professor Art - Emeritus
Morehead State University
Morehead, Kentucky

OLD-FASHIONED FOURTH

Pete Peterson

OLD-FASHIONED FOURTH

The flames that ate baby sister Mandy alive and turned Pap to a black cinder, left me scarred ugly and burned away my talk box. Ain't nobody knows how the fire started, nor where my Momma's at. I live today 'cause of Miss Ethel's nursin'. Pap said always pay yer debts, so I'll let the ladies gander at me if that's what she want desires.

Last night she said, "You'll have a dinger of a good time in Yellowbird tomorrow. There's a parade, with shootin' guns and ya can eat fried chicken and apple pie and ice cream 'til ya bust." That must be how ya celebrate the birthday of our nation, the good ole U.S. of A. I ain't up on what all that but when Pap lived he taken me and Mandy and Mom to a shindig down river to St. Charles that were most likely the same sort of shenanigans, with boys throwin' fire crackers to skeer dogs and cause horses to go wild-eyed.

It were loud Mandy wet herself. She crawled onto my lap and hid her face in my overalls, her stubby fingers holdin' on like a baby possum to its momma's tail.

When it got quiet and blue smoke smellin' like gun powder hung in the holler, Pap went to feed the mules. Mom seen her chance and skipped off to a speakeasy. Three days later she come back, smellin' like piss and whiskey, her face swole up and gray as a wasp's nest. Pap laid her in the wagon and give her biscuits and warm milk to eat. She'd puke and cuss, swearin' she'd had her last drink.

Come daylight, we hit the road hopin' she'd honor her pledge and we'd rent a house, plant a garden, and me and Mandy go to school like regular folks.

Now Miss Ethel says, "Hamas, take off that hat so folks get a good look at ya." I wear one of Ryman's old caps she sewed lace to that shields the sun from my scars and hide my ugliness. I jam it into my pocket, though without it I feel plum nekkid. If Pap were here, me and him would go fishin' and I'd not be sport for the ladies.

Miss Ethel says, "Ryman found him in a hollow oak, bad burned and near froze to death. The fire snuffed out his daddy and baby sister, may they rest in peace. His momma too, though she mighta wondered off and the animals ate her. We ain't rightly sure, since we ain't found her bones."

These stiff necks don't give a handful of mulberries if Momma's dead or alive, since she weren't they's type. These gals would no more drink beer if they's well ran dry than they'd loan a neighbor a spoon of brown sugar. Beer were Momma's favorite drink next to rye whiskey.

Miss Ethel turns me this way and that. A lady touches my face. "Feels kinda like a lizard don't it?" Another says, "It's a miracle of the Lord Jesus you're alive today."

She could be right. Still and all, I'm glad Miss Ethel were around to put salve on my burns and spoon warm soup down my gullet and do nursin' things that got me on the road to mendin'. I ain't sayin' Jesus wouldn't adone it, just that he weren't here and Miss Ethel were.

When the ladies' ooh's and ah's slow, Miss Ethel leads me to a bench under a big elm. "Wait here till I fetch you for eats," and she goes back to the church group. It were last January when Ryman found me. I ain't been alone once since then, 'cept nights. I take a deep breath and close my eyes. Bein' laughin' stock for the ladies tuckered me out.

If Mandy were here, she'd cup her stubby hands around my face, and look at me in the kindest way with her Chinaman's eyes. I wish I could've saved her from that dang fire, but she was ablaze afore I got to her.

Women voices come from the tent behind me. Probably ladies rustlin' up grub for the feast later. A young'un squalls from a nearby wagon and a bob white whistles. A fire cracker explodes.

"Look at this can," a boy calls. "It's bent all to shit." A man yells, "Ya'll blow off a hand tyin' them M-80's together. Take your mischief elsewhere afore I call the constable."

A breeze stirs the leaves, causin' ghosts and goblins to chase across the dirt beneath the elm. On the road, me and Mandy's bed roll was under the wagon.

Sometimes a hoot owl would call from a tree, lonely and forlorn, sendin' a chill up my spine. The fire snaps like a broke bone, shootin' sparks to die in the black air. I shiver and hide my head under the blanket.

I were asleep when 2 small boys, run up, eager as pups explorin' the world.

"Whatcha sittin' here for?"

I can't answer.

They eye me. The biggest one wrinkles his forehead.

"What happened to you? Your face is red as blood."

He leans close, like a horse reachin' for grass through a wire fence. His nose most touches mine. I give him a loud hiss. He jumps like a yellow jacket stung him and runs off, screechin'. The other boy, bellers and chases after him, dust flyin' from bare heels.

I settle my hat and doily over my eyes and wiggle down. 'Fore sleep comes, I've got visitors agin. The boys are back, bringin' other fellers with 'em. They sneak up on all fours, like Injun braves huntin' buffalo. I'm used to bein' the freak, so I sit straight actin' like I don't see 'em.

A tall boy, with a shock of blonde hair touches my shoulder. "What happened to you? Was you scalded or somethin'?"

I nod.

"Yer the ugliest sombitch I ever seen." He smells like hay and sweat. "I bet you're a asshole, too."

Quick, like a water moccasin strikes a mouse, he snatches my hat. This riles me, I tell you. I'd fight 'em, but it's six to one, with them six.

"Here's yer hat, Scarecrow." He shakes it in my face. I grab for it. He tosses it to a boy behind him.

"Look at this girly lace," he says. He grabs a handful of dirt and throws it in my face. "Now ya can't see, nor talk."

My eyes sting and fill with tears. If I had a club, I'd whack 'em all.

"Cry baby, cry baby. See the baby cry."

Rough hands jerk me to my feet, pinnin' my arms to my side. I spin once, twice, five times, grow dizzy and fall in the dust. The boys laugh and yell. It ain't fun for me, I tell you.

A red-headed boy pulls a egg from his overalls. "Hey,

everybody. Watch me. I'll crown him king."

He pretends he's a radio announcer. "And now, dear listeners, come along as I christen 'Scarecrow, King of the 'Uglies.'" His egg cracks agin my head like a blacksnake whip. Egg innards, warm as snot, slide off my head, seep under my shirt, ooze down my belly and plop on the ground between my bare feet. All I do is squirm.

The boys shout. "Give him a parade. Give him a parade." Another egg splats agin my head.

"Hey. What's goin' on here?" It's a grown-up voice. I recognize it as Ryman's, Miss Ethel's husband. "Wondered what the ruckus was all 'bout."

He grabs the boy who just broke an egg on my head. "What's yer name?"

"Ed Standis."

"Yer daddy, Hiram Standis?"

"Yes, sir." He's tunin' up to cry.

"Go get him. I want a word."

A passel of men have come up, probably drawn by the boy's whoops.

"That's him." He points to a stubble-faced feller.

"Hiram, get over here."

Hiram Standis sidles up. He wears clean overalls and a new straw hat.

"I just seen somethin' that makes my blood boil. Yer boy broke a egg on this feller's skull. He's family Ethel's been nursin'. That rubs me wrong, I tell ya."

Hearin' Ryman call me family is a jolt. I'm just charity he's given bed and board to.

Hiram Standis says, "Now, Ryman, they's just boys havin' fun."

"Fun? When's bein' pelted with hen eggs fun? How'd

ya like it if I broke one on yer head?"

Hiram Standis shrugs. "Fellers raggin' each other. No harm done."

"Ya a bird brain, Hiram. Yer boy apologizes or I'll bang ya both with somethin' harder'n eggs."

"Now Ryman, hold on. Ain't no reason to get fired up."

"This a one-sided game, Hiram. When does my feller get a turn? I'm gonna whup yer ass 'less yer boy says sorry."

Ryman's hand is on my shoulder. "This boy's had a run of bad luck that would kill most folks, but he's got more guts than a turkey buzzard. Last week he weren't strong enough to go to the privy. Today, he's at a Fourth of July celebration."

Hiram eyes Ryman like a auctioneer sizes up a prize bull, his face white as peeled cucumber. Ryman stands solid as a corner fence post, his fists fryin' pan big.

Hiram turns to his son. "Ya shouldn't a done what ya done. Boy. Make apology." Hiram slips into the crowd. "Ain't kids sumthin'? Never know what they's next trick is."

The men drift off. Ryman makes us boys shake hands all 'round and all 'cept me say sorry. That over, Ryman says, "Parade's startin'. Let's go."

* * *

The men all hold guns, standin' side-by-side. The town constable and a top dog from Yellowbird Bank and his wife are up front. The constable says, "Listen up.The pretty lady'll drop her handkerchief, then I'll call ready, aim, fire. Yo' all raise your gun and shoot three times. Squeeze 'em off together, okay?"

Fourteen-year-old Grover Cleveland, represents the

Call family. He crackles like a guinea hen when he shoots his gun smilin' at the fiercesome noise them shot guns make. Then he stands, gun stock on the ground while a 6-piece band screeches out what passes for music.

A boy, my size beats a drum. Another feller waves a stick. The band tootles "Dixie", a song folks 'round here like a lot. Two old men wearin' gray uniforms trimmed in a yeller with a coat that has two rows of shiny buttons down the front come forward. The crowd claps and yells, "Hip, hip, hurrah. Hip, hip, hurrah." They shout this three times.

Miss Ethel says, "These gentlemen fought in the Silver War. Ain't many heroes like 'em left nowadays."

That war musta been some time ago, cause these fellers are wrinkled and stove up with age. Pap told me oncet the Silver War were a bad go all around. It sure ain't my idee of fun. Pap said sons fought daddies and brother went agin brother. That sounds plum silly to me. If I went agin Pap he'd mash me like a bug he were so strong.

One of the old gentleman stands out front all by hisself. He yells, "Attention. Katy's count. Forward, march."

The men start to march. The old feller goes, "Hip, two, three, four. Hip, two, three, four." And the men do the same. They march down past the wagons and back, twicet. When they stop, a fat man blows his horn. Four men in witch hats, wearin' white bed sheets that cover them head to toe, come up. I know they're men from the shoes they wear. They wave a red, white and blue flag with a big blue X on it, and white stars in the X.

. Ida Mae, Miss Ethel's oldest daughter, says, "The Klu Klux Klan with the Confederate flag. Don't they know its July 4th, 1933, not 1863?"

A white sheet man waves a Bible. "Let us pray." From

how he carries on you'd think he had God on wages. He says Jesus hates them who mingle with the coloreds and the white race better watch out or else niggers will soon vote and go to school with our precious little ones and sainted white ladies will be locked away to protect their sacred womanhood. I ain't up on why he prays all this, only that he did.

When he finally shuts up, the white sheet fellers strut off to claps and whistles and the tall feller in the grey coat yells, "Attention." The men stick out they's chest and tuck in they's chin. A boy with a bad case of sweats blows what Ida Mae says is "Taps." That ends the parade and the feast starts.

* * *

I load up on fried chicken and biscuits and cream corn. Grover Cleveland leans over and whispers, "Dummy, think yo' momma found herself a black man now yo' Daddy's dead?"

Ryman says, "Hush, Grover. Don't talk to yer brother like that, hear?" This takes me aback, but I can't say nothin' Grover rolls his eyes, "Can I show folks my turtle?"

Yestriddy, he caught a big snapping turtle on his trot-line. He brung it along in Miss Ethel's wash tub. I know trot-lines since Pap were a everday fisherman. It's just heavy string with hooks danglin' down ever 3 or 4 feet. You bait the hooks with worms or minnows, then knot one end of the trot-line to a stake or tree, stretch it across a creek or river and tie it at the other end.

Grover Cleveland's fishin' spot's too wide for his line to reach clean across, so he knots it to a saplin' fifty feet or so out. He poles out in his skiff twice a day to pull in fish and rebait. Mostly, he catches catfish or drum and buffalo. He sells them to neighbors or town folks. Sometimes, he hooks a big turtle.

Ryman says, "Go on. But no egg fights. Keep outta Dark Town, hear?"

That were good advice, but I'm afraid it didn't take with Grover. Nor me.

* * *

The music hits when I'm in the clearin', its sound sweet as honey. My feet go heel and toe like a puppet on a string. Folks have gathered under what Pap would call a brush arbor, tree limbs laid over forked poles set in the ground.

Under a tall sycamore, 2 colored men make music. They laugh and cut up so you can tell they's havin' a grand time. They swig from a Mason jar and hop around like grass hoppers on a leaf. All folks here is colored.

Kiss my wrist. I'm in Dark Town, where Ryman said don't go. I plop down next to a lilac bush with a clear look at the music makers, but I can't sit still, the music is so darn good. On most songs, the guitar player strums, sings and blows the hand organ. Angels ride the fiddler's bow, his music's so fine. They play a mournful song, followed by a happy one, with no stoppin' between tunes.

A cigar box sets on a hay bale. Folks drop pennies or nickels in it from time-to-time.The musicians nod at this. That's they's wages, I figure. I'd yell and holler, if I could, but all can do is jig like I got new shoes. The musicians smile and point at me.

I figure if I ain't welcome here a darky'd tell me to move on. Not one comes up to gander at my scars. When I were on the road with Pap, we'd run onto colored folk's right often. The only difference between them and us that I could see, was they ate better. Sometimes, a friendly lady would cut me a hunk of corn bread with a slice of bacon or maybe a chicken back, which I were most grateful for. Mandy too, since I'd share.

Now, 2 young ladies, dresses hiked up over they's knees so they're free to wiggle, make the dust rise with fast feet and gyratin' bodies. I reckon if Ryman finds out I here, he'll whup my ass, mebbe make me leave his bed and board, though I figure Miss Ethel wouldn't stand for that. I know it's time to head for the wagon, but my feet just won't go that way.

Howsomever, before you can say Merry Christmas, the sun goes low. The fiddle player says to his audience, "Milkin' time comin' on. This is our last song. Thank yo 'all for lettin' us entertain ya."

After the last note is played, dancers wipe off sweat, give hugs and head for they's mules. Some of 'em put a jar of jelly, loaf of bread or chicken leg next to the cigar box. It hurts my heart for the music to stop. I could gorge on it 'til next Tuesday. I wish I could stay here, safe and music-fed forever.

The guitar player comes up. I'm flummoxed and forget I can't talk. I squeal and point at him. He laughs. "I'm Harry. That's my brother Hob with the fiddle."

He bows low. "We 'preciate yer comin'. Now be off to whoever brung ya."

I reach in my pocket and take out the nickel Miss Ethel given me earlier to spend anyhow I see fit and hand it to him.

"Ain't no need for that."

I bow like he did earlier, hands under my chin. Folks have to learn, Hamus Zanderhook pays his way. Harry's brown eyes search mine. He takes my nickel. "Much obliged, friend. Now go."

I head at a fast gait toward the bridge. I disregarded Miss Ethel's instructions comin' here. She said when my nap were over to come to the big tent. Pap always said it were a good idee to know where you was, so if you come back agin, you'll know where you been.

So with sleep in my eyes, I hop down from the wagon and head toward the railroad tracks. Two girls at the next wagon stop the hand slap game and look at me like I'm lice in little brother's hair. The girl in the blue dress covers her mouth. The yellow dress girl rolls her eyes. They both snicker. I walk.

A foot bridge crosses a crick jist past the tracks. On the other side, a path leads to a clearin'. That's where Hob and Harry's music hits me and reason leaves my mind. Now, headed for the wagon, at the bridge, Grover Cleveland runs up. He carries Miss Ethel's tub. It's empty.

Grover says, "Yer in Dark Town, Dummy. Daddy said don't come here. I'm gonna tell." He laughs. "Yo' ain't got no more meat on you'n a coat hanger, but darkies will boil it off and eat ya anyway."

He sees me glance at the empty tub. "Sold it for seventy-five cents." He says the money amount real slow.

"I give a pickaninny a dime, took her down to the culvert and did a job on her. I won't get a stiffy for a week." He laughs and runs off.

I cross the bridge. My heart about stops. Sittin' on a stump like a gray wolf waitin' for a fat rabbit, is Granny Krebs, a widder woman who comes and goes like chokeberries in the spring, or sleet in the winter. She reads tea leaves and brags she can forecast storms and divine the future. I ain't seen her since the day afore our shack burned down.

"'Member me," she asks.

I nod.

Folks claim Granny carries a haunt, that if she visits at calfin' time, you'll have a calf born with two heads. If you eat chicken and dumplings for supper and she's at your table, you'll burn dead chickens within the week.

"I seen ya with them darkies." Her laugh is a loud cackle. "They don't mind ugly folks, I reckon."

She draws on her pipe. "It's a miracle of the Lord Jesus Christ you're alive."

I nod.

"Seen yer momma?"

I shake no. Like most everone, I figure she knows Momma ain't been seen since the fire.

"When I come by yo' all's cabin the night 'fore it burnt, yer cupboard were bare as flint stone. I come back the next day with a mess of squirrel stew and grits. Only ashes where yer cabin stood. I seen things there that make chills go up my back."

Granny's pale blue eyes seem to look through me. "Let me warn ya. She's alive. She started that fire sure as a skunk's black. Ya owe me, boy. I given yer dead Pap and little sister a Christian burial. Thank ya, Lord Jesus Christ."

Granny knocks ash from her pipe. "Where yer Momma is, I ain't divined, but she'll cause ya travail for years to come."

Then, like a spider web blowin' in the wind, she disappears into the trees. Leavin' me with prickles up my back. I run for the wagon.

* * *

Now that we're headed home, I figure Grover'll brag

about how he sold his turtle, but he dangles his feet off the back of the wagon, silent as a toad frog. Then it comes to me. If he says he got money for it, Ryman'll make him share with his sisters. Charity ain't Grover's way.

My heart slows some. I rest agin the wagon sideboard, swayin' when it goes over a bump. The thud of mule's hooves on the dirt makes my eyes heavy.

Miss Ethel speaks up. "It were a fine day, even if Hiram Standis showed his red ass. What'd you call him, Ryman? A bird brain?" We all laugh. She goes quiet.

Grover Cleveland whispers, "I'm gonna tell I seen ya in Dark Town soon's we're home."

Ida Mae hears him. "Grover, where's yer turtle?"

"Turned it loose in the crick."

She laughs. "No way. I figure a black family's gonna have turtle soup for supper."

* * *

Hob and Harry's music swirls in my head. I hope someday to play a musical instrument so fine that when I strike the first note, folks'll smile and be happy. I know this is jist a dream. I don't have a instrument to play, nor voice box to sing with. Still, Pap said a feller could always hope. That's what I'll do. Hope and hope and hope. That way mebbe I'll forget Granny Krebs' warnin' about my momma and only have Grover Cleveland to worry on.

The End

EMBERS THAT LINGER SO

EMBERS THAT LINGER SO

"The worst that can happen is they kill us," Elva says. That ain't my wish, but good folks do bad things when hard times hit, and hard times are here and these boys know hard times.

I nod. If I could talk, I'd say, "It were yer idee, Girl."

Me and Elva want to see these boys carry the grub we bought 'em home, not sell it or be robbed 'fore they can feed they's family. We cross the cemetery, climb a barbwire fence, follow a path through rag weeds, buckbrush and persimmon sprouts, to a lean-to under two big sycamore trees at the bend in the creek.

A woman sprawls in the dirt, her head restin' on a battered foot locker. Her dress top sags open, her face pale as flint rock. Flies have a go at her mouth, but she pays 'em no mind. A baby nekkid as the day she were born, kicks and squirms on a dirty blue blanket 'side the lady.

"This is mostly where we stay," the oldest boy says, kickin' at a clump of dead grass with a dirty tennis shoe.

The lean-to is a paint-splotched tarpaulin draped over a tree limb, slopin' down in back, tied to stobbs hammered in the ground. The sides are mostly gunny sacks thrown over ropes and held by rocks. The front's open to the air 'cept for a blanket threaded on a rope they pull shut to give a little privacy come bed time.

Under a nearby sycamore, a boy and his dog crawl out of a cardboard shack low to the ground. A woman stirrin' a fire says, "Lovelle, stay out that swimmin' hole today, hear. And go to school. Don't want to bury a drowned boy like that momma last week."

"Yes, Ma," he answers, in a low voice. He gives me and Elva a hard stare, but don't nod. A older feller, his leg twisted 'round a hickory sapling, his face hid by a straw hat, leans agin a sycamore to get his wind 'fore he hops off toward a tin-roof shanty growin' in the weeds. Six or eight more cardboard and scrap wood huts, blister the area like ugly wasps nests. We're in Hooverville, where folks don't live, just hang on.

These places commenced when Herbert Hoover were president, but nowadays, Franklin D. Roosevelt's the top dog in Washington, D.C. Still, things ain't changed much though the newspapers say F.D.R.'s Works Progress Administration gave men jobs that ended the Great Depression. Folks here must not read the news.

Inside the lean-to, the only household goods I see are two flatirons on the footlocker, a folded ironin' board next to a cane rocker and a rickety-lookin' cot with a wadded up green blanket. Outside, a white enamel chamber pot – what Pap called a thunder mug – lies in the grass. They's privy, I reckon.

The boy who panhandled us first, points to the woman

in the dirt. "That's Momma. She's sick two days. Baby's Suella." He puts a hand 'side his mouth and yells, "Joan, where are ya?"

A tousled-headed girl, eleven or twelve, curled in the rocker so deep I took her for bed clothes, stands. Her blue dress most drags the ground. A man's tie, decorated with blue and yellow flowers, dangles from her neck. She wears heavy, scuffed boots that make her legs look thin as a spider.

The oldest boy says, "She ain't feelin' so hot, neither."

Elva says, "Hi everyone," likes she's greetin' cash-payin' customers at the Upstairs Diner where me and her work. "Nice to meet you."

She looks at Joan. "Where's your cooking pot, Hon?"

Joan, who I take is the older sister, jerks her head toward a fire ring behind the lean-to.

Elva asks, "Water?"

Joan points to a glass butter churn. She has a pretty face, with eyes black as fresh-hulled walnuts and hair yellow like wind-blown chaff.

Elva pours water from the churn into a pan, dumps in stew makin's, and hands it to me. I kick the char off a log and start a fire usin' butcher paper as kindlin'.

When it flames yellow, the younger boy adds small twigs. "Ya got that goin' in a hurry," he says. "Tried all mornin' with no luck."

The older boy tosses a chunk of wood into the fire. Embers come to life and set things ablaze. He looks at me. "Had us a fire with nothin' to cook last night."

When the flames go good, I settle the stew pot between two rocks, then go inside the lean-to to help Elva with sandwiches. Me and her ate at the Upstairs after our shift, so we ain't hungry.

The older boy shakes his momma awake. She snatches the 7-Up and takes a long swig. "Anythin' fer Suella?"

"Yes, Momma. Sit up. We got company. They brung eats."

Baby Suella kicks and whimpers. The lady scoops her up and skootches closer to the rocker.

Elva hands out sandwiches, then crouches next to the footlocker. "These'll hold you 'til the stew's ready."

From the dirt, the lady says, "Ya caught us at a bad time. Me sick and all." Her hand hides her mouth. "If I'd knowed company were comin', I'd swept and had the boys get in fresh water."

Elva says, "Don't worry, ma'am. Hamus and I don't expect fancy." She looks 'round. "You got a man?"

The oldest boy, his voice low like he's tellin' secrets says, "Pap took off outta here last week like we was three-headed ghosts with polio. Momma don't want to think on it, but he's gone fer good. Stole my ball cap right off my head."

The woman gums her sandwich, then with long fingers, takes a gob of chewed food from her mouth and pushes it 'tween Suella's lips. "Eat, chile."

Her voice is hoarse like she ain't talked in a while. "Yeah, Ralph took off. Week Wednesday." I figure Ralph to be her husband.

"Cain't say I blame him. Livin' in dirt with no roof over yer head and six mouths to feed. His ass was red that this were the best he could do, though his lazy ways brung us here. Mr. Perfect never done one thing wrong to hear him yammer."

She takes 'nother gulp of 7-Up. "Nah, he ain't comin' back."

She puts a strand of hair behind her ear, and glances at me. "How'd yer man git so bad scarred?"

Elva answers. "House fire when little. Burned away his voice box. He can't talk, but he's a good man."

"Didn't say he weren't. We all got our cross to bear. That's his'n, I reckon." Her voice holds tears. "Hope Mr. High and Mighty Ralph finds his life's treasure, since we ain't good 'nuff fer him. He's partial to hard drink and soft work. Left me in a big hole, he did fer sure."

She takes a breath. "Reckon the boys can fend for themselves. It's Joan I worry on." She swallows. "Young girls got problems boys ain't got, though life's hard for all of God's childrun."

She pushes more chewed sandwich into Suella's mouth. "Joan's time ain't come yet but will soon. Men sniffin' 'round already. And no daddy to protect her."

Joan, balled up in the rocker agin, sits up, looks 'round, wipes her hands on her dress, then falls back in the chair.

Her momma says, "I weren't ready 'til I met they's Pop, but he weren't my first." She glances at the boys. "'Nuff said."

Suella whimpers. Her momma picks her up. "It were right Christian of ya to stop by. Come agin when the garden's ready. We'll fix green beans and new 'taters. Quilt, if we got lamp oil."

Her mention of a garden makes me roll my eyes. I ain't seen a hill of beans or a 'tater vine nowhere.

Elva says, "Let's go, my man." She pinches my wrist when she says this.

The brothers follow us up the hill. A gaggle of scruffy-lookin' hooligans watch from the shadows, probably drawn by the smell of cookin' meat and onions.

A boy yells, "Ya owe me, Willard. I give ya some of my Fudgesicle yestriddy."

Willard must be the oldest boy's name. He picks up a thick stick. "Leave us be, Leo. Momma's sick. Joan, too."

"It's charity yer takin'," Leo yells. "Ya ain't got no Daddy."

A man in overalls covered in paint, his face dark with whiskers, a leather hat hidin' his eyes, says, "Don't give a shit if it's from the devil. Food's food. Me an' mine are hongry." He waves eatin' utensils. "We ain't eit since Sunday."

The question of when the last time somebody ate, is why me and Elva is here. Me and Elva finished our ten-hour shift at the Upstairs Café where she's a Soup Jockey and me, Grill Master. I were on my way to see Abe when Elva asked could she walk with me.

Now, Abe Bedford's the best piano player the world's ever heard, and my friend. 'Fore his Granny died, Abe held concerts in London, Paris, France, even New York City. It were a lucky day for us Music Freaks, the band we cripples put together, when Abe joined up.

His name alone landed us a radio show and we played honky-tonk jobs all 'cross Cole County. A month or so back, Abe come up sick.

That's my concern 'cause the Bank Lady, Miss Duncan, hired me to see that Abe eats right and don't stay up all night playin' music like he's been known to do. I don't take one red cent for helpin' him. After all, what are friends for. I do bed down in a back room of his house even if he is colored and me white.

Last night were a bad one for Abe. I put him down 'round nine, he got up two hours later and commenced to play Happy Birthday over and over on his piano. For over a hour, he'd play a few notes of one song, then skip to 'nother one without finishin' either. I coaxed him to bed three times, but this mornin' found him slouched on his piano bench, his face wet with drool, his skin ashy. It were a struggle to put him down agin, I tell you.

At my mornin' break at the Upstairs, I ran to the bank to tell Miss Duncan that Abe needs a doctor, like I've been instructed to do. "Abe's heart is bad," I wrote on my paper. "Send for a doctor."

Miss Duncan read my scribbles. "Mr. Zanderhook, I had no idea a fry cook like you diagnosed illnesses as well. Leave by the side door, right now, before a bank officer sees you. I'll send Dr. Staley by to see Mr. Bedford as his schedule permits."

I want Elva to know what Miss Duncan said. Me and her have worked side-by-side at the Upstairs four years now. She comes to our dances right regular and is up on the fact that the Music Freaks voted to not play any more dances or be on the radio again 'til Abe's up and 'round.

I'll write what happened at the bank on my paper once we're at Abe's, 'cause when me and Elva talk, she sometimes don't understand my grunts, hisses, face looks and hand gestures so good. Writin' what happens is better.

When Elva asked could she walk with me, I were taken aback, I tell you. She's pretty as a violet, friendly as a wren. She and her boyfriend, Bill Weir, are to be married soon. Some nights Elva rides up front when Howard Wilson drives me and Abe and Stumpy Hazlet, who has no legs, but plays the fire outta a guitar, and our singer, polio-crippled, sweet-voiced Della Holt, to our dance jobs. Howard hisself, has a wood arm. To play his fiddle, he pins the bow to his stub so the bow makes the music he wants.

I figure Elva wants to tell Abe get well, so I nod my okay. It's a fine October evenin' with air crisp as a fresh apple.

While we stroll, Elva tells me her sister's feelin' poorly agin and her Momma bought canning jars with the five-dollar bill Elva given her last week. At the Little Red Store, on Ozark Street, most to Abe's house, this kid, whose name I now know is Willard, sidled up.

"Hey, Mister, could you spare three cents for a 7-Up? Momma's sick two days, and a 7-Up would make her better, I betcha."

The younger boy looks on. Elva asks them, "When did you last eat?"

"We have a big bait most every day," the older boy says. His tennis shoes make his feet look long. His sweat shirt is faded red and could use a good scrubbin'. His hair ain't combed, but don't look bad.

Elva turns to the other boy. "You his brother?"

He nods.

Elva takes his arm. "Don't lie. When was your last meal?"

He looks down at the dirt. "Two, three days ago." He puts his hands up, like he expects a hard wallop from big brother, but it don't come. He's barefoot, wears a St. Louis Browns ball cap and overalls two sizes too big. He ain't too acquainted with soap and water neither.

Elva says, "Wait here."

She's inside the store, fast. I motion to the boys I'll be back and follow her. The light is dim inside, with the smell of apples and coffee and candle wax. We fill four sacks with groceries.

Outside, Elva gives each boy a sack and me and her carry one, too. "We'll follow you home," she says.

I'd rather we'd go check on Abe, who is sick, but can't let Elva go by herself.

That were a hour or so ago. Now, we stand on a narrow path in Hooverville with mad, hungry men blockin' our way. "We're hongry, too," a bean pole of a boy says.

The man in the flat hat who spoke up earlier says, "Guarantee ya. Me and mine are gonna bait up tonight."

A woman with a blue bandanna 'round her head, wearin' a red and blue apron, pushes through the crowd.

"Wilmer Ray Burks, ya an' yer sister Elizabeth Irene, git over here. We ain't so poor ya havta beg fer handouts. Yer Daddy'll feed ya come mornin'. Evenin' for shore." She pulls both kids up the hill.

Mr. Flat Hat says to Elva, "I'll take that stew, ma'am. It'd cook just fine over my fire."

"You'd steal from a family with a sick momma?"

"Ain't my momma who's sick. Mine died a year ago, Girly."

Elva whispers, "Hamus, go get the rest of the groceries."

When I'm back with two bags, she says to Flat Hat, "You talk like a leader. Take these. See everyone gets some. Leave these folks alone."

He grabs the sacks. "Ya got it, Pretty Girl."

He eyes me up and down. "Think a scarred-up banjo player who plays music with a darkie can keep me from takin' ya if I want?"

"You recognize him, huh," Elva says. "Do something stupid and he'll put it on the radio. Fast. The sheriff'll come and clear this place out. You don't want that. You got your grub. Now, move on."

Flat Hat gives her a long look, then turns. The mob follows him mebbe twenty yards up the hill. Willard asks, "When didja say that stew'd be ready, ma'am?"

"Anytime now," Elva says. "Anytime."

Me and her walk up the hill past the gang. Flat Hat and a man carryin' a baseball bat, are jaw-to-jaw. Bat Man slams the bat agin the ground. "Feelin' froggy, Humphrey? Jump. I'll beat ya shitless."

Flat Hat says, "I didn't say cut ya out. I said, cut my brother and his'n in."

"Same thing."

We follow the path to where it forks, stop and look back. The lean-to is a dark blob in the smoke that's settled like fog in the valley, men black shadows.

Elva says, "Who're we fooling? Our boys won't get one mouthful of that stew. It'll be stolen before we're up the hill."

We wind our way through the tomb stones and cross the street in front of the store where the boys first panhandled us. A man in overalls and shock hat stops us.

"Know where an honest man can get an honest day's pay for an honest day's work?"

Elva says, "No. Sure wish I did."

I reckon that's as good a answer as you can expect from a Soup Jockey and a banjo player. Now, mebbe we can go tend to Abe and his needs.

The End

THE FOOD THIEF

THE FOOD THIEF

Momma always said acid from a lie burns a hole in your heart and turns you into a person no one likes to be around. I reckon that's why Dad and Josephine hate me. I've lied plenty since Momma died from a cottonmouth water moccasin's bite two days before my tenth birthday, last June.

Josephine, who's thirteen and thinks she's going to be a big movie star someday, says, "Jeremy, if you loved Momma like I did, you'd have been there when she went to heaven."

"Onion sauce," I say.

In *The Wind in the Willows,* the River Rat says this when he's fed up with stupid things. Momma whispered it to me one Sunday when the preacher said you'd go to Hell if you read anything other than the Bible.

I say to Josephine what I've said a hundred times, "Momma knew I was at a spelling bee. She was proud I was the only boy on the team."

Josephine ignores this. "Our Momma died June the 8th, in the year of Our Lord, Nineteen Hundred and Fifty-One, while you were wasting time spelling words. It was I who held her hand her last minutes on this earth." Her brown eyes go wet and big.

More onion sauce. If Dad had been home like a good husband should've been, he could have taken Momma to a doctor and she'd be alive today.

For the hundredth time this week, Josephine says, "Momma was pukin' something awful when me and Dad put her in the truck and Dad drove like a maniac to get her to the doctor, her arm purple as calf's liver." She folds her hands like Preacher Wilson at Yellowbird Baptist does when he talks about sinners. "You should be ashamed of yourself, Jeremy Holt. Your momma died, and you were off having fun."

I'd like to smack her face but walk away instead.

* * *

The night before the spelling bee in Jeff City, Momma baked cookies. When Superintendent Diehl stopped his car in front of our house the next morning, I squirmed in between Claudette Wilson and Sara Ann Jameson. Momma handed her cookies to Superintendent Diehl in a brown paper sack tied with a pink ribbon.

"Brain food," she said. "Show 'em how smart you are." The girls thought she was talking to them. I knew she meant me.

* * *

Dad doesn't seem at all bothered that Momma died. He's too busy yelling at me to help turn our forty-acres of rocks and persimmon sprouts in the Missouri Ozarks into a Garden of Eden like he thinks he can do.

"Move it, Jeremy," he yells. "Yer slower 'n a sick cow. We got work to do."

Why bother, I'd like to say. It'd take Albert Einstein all day to count the jars of green beans, tomatoes, snap peas and pickled pears in our cellar. Besides, who's going to put up what we grow, now that Momma's dead?

While I slave in the hot sun, Josephine is upstairs, a cool breeze blowing through open windows, staring into her mirror, makeup caked on her stupid face, red lipstick smeared on her mouth, blonde hair dangling over one eye, saying over and over, "I vant to be left alone."

Does Dad yell it her? Never. It's "Honey this," and "Honey that," even when she won't go near the kitchen, since heat makes her make up run and her face break out. Dad says, "Honey, why don't ya cook 'fore ya put on yer war paint? 'Sides, girls get pimples. Part of growin' up. If you'd just cooperate, thing's would go better."

Dad rattles off a list of chores for me to do, then drives to the Yellowbird Post Office to guzzle Coca Cola and gab with the ladies when they stop by for their mail. He comes home, parks his pickup in the yard around sunset, and steps into the tool shed for a nip of bourbon. Momma wouldn't let liquor of any kind in her house, so Dad hides his bottle there in the rafters. After a snort or two, he yells, "Josephine, honey, supper ready?"

Josephine slams stale Holsum bread, a can of Spam, and yellow mustard on the table. Dad says, "That ain't hardly 'nuff to keep a mouse alive. Honey, ya mope 'round all day agin?"

Josephine bolts upstairs, black tears dripping from her chin. Dad studies his shoes then says, "Jeremy, fry me some eggs. With bacon."

Folks pay Dad cash money to change suckers on a well pump chain, fix a sagging gate, or replace rotten boards in a kitchen floor, but at home, he's hobo lazy. I told him last month's windstorm blew tin off the back-porch roof. He said, "I'll get to it directly, Jeremy. Now, we've more important things to do."

I try again. "The screen door needs a new spring, and the hoe handle's busted."

"Damn, boy! Ya hector worse'n yer momma. Do what I say. Compost my tomatoes and cut them horse weeds down by the ash tree so we can plant cabbage there come fall."

Why this has to be done is a mystery, since Dad probably won't see it when I'm finished. His favorite trick is to disappear for 3-4 days at a time. Once, when Momma was alive, I waited in bed for her to come in and sing, "Joy shall be yours in the morning," like the field mice do in *Willows.*

When she didn't come in, I ran outside thinking she was in the garden. All I got was cold wet dew on my bare feet. Momma was sitting in the dark kitchen, drinking cold coffee, her eyes red as clay. "Jeremy, your Daddy smells out white-livered ladies wherever he goes," she said. "His slow smile and brown calf's eyes whisper he knows a lady's wants and they lift their skirts.That's my cross to bear."

* * *

On my eleventh birthday last week, Josephine gave me a rusty knife she found in the tool shed, wrapped it in paper from a Big Chief notebook and wrote, "Happy Brithday, little Brother." She's in the eighth grade, but spells worse than a third grader.

I was oiling my ball glove on the back porch when Dad came home. "Yer eleven now, Jeremy. Yer growed. It were a bad break yer momma died, but time to move on. I'd adopt ya out, but no one wants a boy as ugly as you, so yer mine. I tell ya, Boy, from now on, things are gonna change 'round here."

He points to two cardboard boxes on the porch steps. "Yer momma's stuff. Take 'em up to that gully past the barn and bury 'em."

I turn to walk away.

"Ya hear me, Boy?"

His face is red. "Yes, sir," I say.

"I'm easy on ya, Jeremy. Hell, in Africa, I could sell ya and ya'd dig gold in a dark hole the rest of yer life. Or, a jungle tribe would pay ten dollars fer ya to herd cows. Do what I say, Boy. Quick. I got more chores when this one's finished."

I nod. "Yes, sir. May I be excused?" Momma said gentlemen always say that when they want to get away.

Cobwebs wave from the tool shed rafters as I pull the wheelbarrow outside. When I was a boy, I'd sit there and cry. Now that I'm a man, I swallow the hurt in my throat, pile Momma's clothes on the wheelbarrow and push it up to the gully, toss her dresses and shoes in the ditch and shovel in dirt.

Her favorite blue sweater, the one she wore to church or to town on Market Day, catches my eye. I hug it close. Her smell dries my tears. I hide this treasure under the porch for nights when I'm home alone and monsters moan in the grape arbor and ghosts flit from room-to-room and my screech owl calls and fox barks won't scare 'em away.

* * *

Dad asks, "Bury everthing?"

"Yes sir."

What did Momma say about lies? I already don't like me.

"Good. Now, load all our canned goods into my truck. I'm tradin' 'em to Corrie Ann Pannell so she'll do our washin' ever two weeks. I ain't wore a clean shirt since yer Momma died."

Corrie Ann Pannell is a black lady with blue eyes, who lives in a tarpaper shanty next to the bridge over Sandy Creek. The first Saturday after we buried Momma, Dad and I stopped at Hord's Grocery to buy matches and P & G soap. Men sat on nail kegs and sacks of seed corn, chewing tobacco, smoking pipes waiting for the Grand Ole Opry to start, their shiny eyes watching Corrie Ann's every move as she dodged garden plows, hunting gear and chicken wire to pile Old Judge coffee, Martha White flour and S&H Cane Sugar into her grocery box.

Corrie Ann wears her blue hat with the red feather, a brown dress and what Mom would call a yellow sash. Her legs are long as a post hole digger, brown as pie crust. Her feet bare, with chipped red nail polish on her toes. Lal Hord totals her bill. "That's four dollars and forty-seven cents, young lady."

Corrie Ann reaches into her bosom and pulls out dollar bills wrapped in a rubber band. She counts out five ones and puts her change into a small red purse dangling from a string around her throat, lifts her tow sack and crosses to the door like music's playing. She turns, nods and steps out on the porch.

Fat Ol' Earl Benny Fitzgerald slaps his knee. "Wooie! That gal keeps her valuables next to her treasures. I'd let her change my luck if she'd ask right nice."

The men whoop. I don't understand this talk. Dad

follows Corrie Ann. "I'll hold yer things while ya mount up, Missy."

Earl Benny slaps his knee. "Ain't that Buller Holt somethin'? His wife not cold in her grave and his pecker's throbbin' for a colored gal."

* * *

I load every single jar of Momma's canned goods into the pickup. Dad climbs in behind the wheel. "Jeremy, first thing tomorrow, pile them boards from the old barn next to the fence and spade the ground so we can plant winter crops this fall. Ya can play after that."

Josephine pipes up from the porch. "I'll bring him sweet tea and samwiches, Daddy."

That winds my clock. "Know what you can do, Blondie? Fix some fried chicken, or roast beef with brown potatoes like Momma used to do."

Josephine's face melts. She's up the stairs two at a time.

Dad says, "Now ya done it, Jeremy. She's still tender from her Momma's passin'."

I'd like to yell, "She was my momma, too." But now that I'm grown, he'd say, "Gonna cry, Little Boy? Want me to fix ya a sugar tit?"

* * *

The sun hides in the sassafras and sumac bushes along the fence line Monday morning. Josephine plops soggy oatmeal and black bacon on the table. Dad swallows a bite or two, then hurries out to his pickup and jounces off to hang a door, lay linoleum or paint a house. After a hot breakfast at the Yellowbird Café, that is.

His truck is barely past the low-water bridge when Josephine disappears to her mirror, makeup and movie magazines. I grab my stealing sack. I need eats. The neighbors have plenty.

* * *

When Momma lived, and I was going somewhere, she'd cup her red hands around my face and whisper, "Jeremy Holt, you're smarter than a Catholic priest."

Now, I head for the Holtzhoutzer house two ridges over. At pie suppers and school pot lucks, folks line up for Amy Holtzhoutzer's cooking. She just had a baby, so she'll prize her chickens for poached eggs and chicken broth. My plan is to hide behind the wash kettle near her hen house and make sounds like a fox raiding her flock. When she hears the commotion, and her husband off in the field, she'll run out, shot gun in hand to protect her pullets. I'll dash around to the back door and help myself to her pantry.

My fox barks and chicken squawks ruin the quiet morning, but Mrs. Holtzhoutzer doesn't come outside to run the fox off. I wait. Then, quiet as a quail in grass, I creep up, and peek in a window. She's slumped in her rocking chair, baby on her shoulder, both sound asleep.

I run around back, slip into her kitchen and fill my jar with green beans and sausage still warm from the stove, wedge a loaf of fresh-baked bread into my sack, grab a jar of honey, then run fast as an Indian for the white oaks along the creek bank.

When my breath slows, I give out fox yips. The food thief strikes. Lies rule.

* * *

Bob and Jenny Zumwalt's house is on my list. They

own the Blue Moon Tavern in Yellowbird, so their pantry should be well-stocked. Their son Eddie was two grades ahead of me in school before he was demoted and stopped coming. I miss him. We'd trade sandwiches, my PB and J's for his roast beef.

A year or so before Momma died, Eddie's hands commenced to shake so he could hardly hold a book. He chews his words before they spill out in a cloud of spit. By Christmas vacation, he's bent and crooked as a hickory limb.

Older boys make sport of him. "Who's blood you gonna suck today?" They play keep away with his cap or lunch box, slobber and curl their arm to mimic him.

Folks says Eddie has The Shakes. Momma says it's multiple sclerosis. "Doesn't affect his mind, just his speech and motor skills. Might be years before full paralysis sets in. Some cases advance faster than others."

That was Momma. She knew everything. She'd read the Book of the Month Club Selection the day the mailman delivered it and spend hours poring over the *Sunday Kansas City Star*. Once she told me, "There are two things you can't hide, Jeremy. Your vocabulary and your grammar. Learn to speak and write like a gentleman, son."

At school, when Eddie's voice is a frog's croak, Mrs. Bassinger demotes him and sits his desk next to mine. He collects homework for our row. One day, picking up papers, he stops, looks at my arithmetic assignment and squawks, "Whee, whee!"

I yank my paper from his claws, and check problem Number Three. My answer is 901. It should be 910. *Ol'Eddie caught that?* I correct my mistake, as he watches, rocking back and forth, sucking three fingers.

Momma was dead and buried when this happened, so

I can't tell her she was right, that Eddie's mind works fine, but not his body. The last time I saw Eddie, he was tied like a criminal next to the boy's privy at school, a bull's eye drawn on his bare chest, smashed persimmons covering his bony arms, a target for the eighth-grade boys. The top scorer wins a kiss from Melinda Kay Rouse. The scar on my lip is where Lloyd Cave busted me when I ratted their game out to Mrs. Bassinger.

Now, I squat behind a juniper tree across the road from the Zumwalt's. There's no pickup in the yard. The house is dark. I race to the wheelbarrow filled with geraniums, lay low and bounce a rock off the screen door. Nothing. I flip a pebble against a window. When no one whoops, or comes outside to look around, I dive into the lilac bushes beside the house, push the window up and drop inside.

Sharp bones jab me. A skull and eyes burning red as charcoal are inches from my nose. I roll over to escape my grave, too scared to yell. In the dim light, there's something familiar about the Halloween mask breathing my air. I'm in bed with my old schoolmate, Eddie.

His parents must have been so ashamed by his paralysis they hid him away, so others wouldn't laugh at their failure. I give him a wave. "Hey, Eddie. How you been?"

His hot eyes dart from my face to an empty glass on the table beside his bed. He squeals and flaps his arms. *Is he thirsty?*

House noises tell me Eddie and I are alone. I fill his glass in the kitchen and hold it while he slurps. Water dribbles from his chin and trickles over his skinny chest and scarecrow ribs. He guzzles two glasses of water, then falls back on dirty sheets.

I've been in outhouses that smell better than in here.

Where does Mrs. Zumwalt keep clean sheets? Momma would put them in a hall closet. I open doors until I find them. Back at his bed, "Eddie, ol' buddy, let's wash up."

Eddie squeals and flaps his arms. It takes all my muscles to get his wooden body from bed to chair. I soap his ball glove-tough skin and stiff legs. Sweat stings my eyes when I strip off shitty sheets. I pull and push to tuck clean sheets over the thin mattress, then slide Eddie back to bed. Their pantry is filled with goodies!

I open a can of fruit cocktail, crumble in graham crackers and spoon this into Eddie's open mouth. He falls to sleep before his lunch is finished. I wipe crumbs from his lips and pull the blanket over his skinny chest. "Sleep tight, my friend."

Outside, near the trash barrel, are four cardboard boxes. I fill them with Quaker Oats and Saltine Crackers, Spam, creamed corn, hominy, and evaporated milk, hide them in the woods then tote out flour, sugar and corn meal. Before my last load, I look in on Eddie. He still sleeps.

Momma taught me to rig a travois, a sled-like contraption Indians used to carry heavy loads. I cut two long saplings for pull poles, tie four stout branches across the poles, pile on my stolen goods, and drag this to the Brandenburg's, where a dozen kids live in a two-room shack. I go to school with Jaybird, when he doesn't ditch. Two broken men, jaws filled with chaw, take the two boxes I carry. I hid the travois loaded with can goods, flour and sugar in the woods, for the Treadway's. Mr. Fred and Miss Alice, are old, maybe sixty or more.

Their house sets on a ridge beneath tall cedars. I pull my load up to the back porch, knock, and hand Miss Alice a five-pound can of coffee when she comes to the door. "I brought you some groceries," I say, stacking two 10-pound sacks of flour, a sack of sugar and three boxes of canned vegetables on the porch. Miss Alice, tears running down her papery face asks, "Where'd you get all this, dear?"

"A grocery truck wrecked out by Slay's Corner," I lie. "They were gonna throw it all away. Thought you might have use for it. Our secret. Okay?"

She looks to the heavens. "Thank you, Sweet Jesus." She touches my arm. "You're a fine young man. What's your name?"

My name? Stan Musial of the Cardinals is my hero. "Stan." Then I remember their famous second baseman, Rogers Hornsby. "Stan Rogers."

"Any kin to Paul Rogers down by Portland?"

"Not that I know of. Excuse me, ma'am, but I gotta run. The preacher needs me to set up chairs for Wednesday night's service." Momma was right. After the first lie, others come easy.

* * *

I live by quick hands and fast feet all summer, but when snow falls, folks hunker down, close doors, lock windows and stay inside to play checkers, plant tomato seeds in tin cans and eat popcorn. When the pantry runs low, the farm wife goes to the root cellar, not the garden. With the lady of the house so close it's hard to steal food. *I may have to settle for Josephine's pimento cheese and stale bread sandwiches, after all.*

Before I stoop that low, I remember root cellars. I case several, just like a bank robber does. Most are shovel-dug into a bank, plastered with cement and lined with boards with dog collars or ropes as handles. Most are located toward the back of the property, away from windows, an easy target for a skilled thief like me.

I hit the Brandt's over by the Cedar Creek bridge, first. When they sit for supper Monday evening, I wrap myself in a bed sheet and inch across snow covered ground, breathing into my sleeve so my warm breath won't form a cloud and give me away. I un-fasten the cellar door, lift, and roll inside where it's warm and smells like fresh dirt and cobwebs.

When my eyes adjust, I fill my sack, sneak out and run foxhound fast to my hideout, my bag crammed with jars of honey, apple sauce, pickled pig's feet, spiced pears, and sauerkraut. *I'll eat like Rockefeller for a week!*

Do I share my goodies with Josephine or Dad? In no way. Snug as a squirrel in a nest, in a lean-to of ash saplings lashed together with grapevines beneath low-growing oak, I gobble beef stew or country-cured ham, fried in butter, with no thought of Josephine's burned baloney cups and tin can spaghetti. I'll take beef chilli and beans, roasted apples drenched with honey, and fresh-baked bread, thank you.

* * *

Summer arrives hot and rainy. At Yellowbird's 4th of July celebration, everyone gabs about the Food Thief. I smile when folks say he's an escaped convict as slick as he is. His animal calls are good some say, others that they don't hear nothing, just that food goes missing.

Josephine asks, "Jeremy, how'd you get beet juice on your shirt? Where did all those empty jars in your sack come from? I'd say you were the Food Thief, 'cept folks say he makes good animal sounds and you can't mimic a cow, much less a fox." Silly girl, Josephine.

I'd still be a happy crook not a teary-eyed Chief Cook and Bottle Washer if two things hadn't happened. First, in

September, Yellowbird held their annual county fair where neighbors show off cattle and geese, lie about how smart their grandkids are and choose what lady makes the best blackberry jam or watermelon rind preserves while scarfing down cotton candy and hot dogs with mustard. Dad drives us to Yellowbird, me hanging on in his pickup's bed, Josephine in Momma's place up front next to Dad, pretty as Lana Turner in a yellow dress, black high heels and long blonde hair.

On the dusty midway, young men and boys gawk, words glued in their throat. Golden-tongued Ray Maxey, twenty-five years old, and handsome in his blue Air Force uniform, says, "Hubba, hubba, Gorgeous. What do we have here?"

"Just little ol' me," Josephine says, her brown eyes shining black.

I watch Ray and Josephine rise up to kiss the moon on the Ferris wheel and wonder if they'll ever come out of the Tunnel of Love. It's so dark there you can't see your own feet. Ol' Ray must have promised Jo the world and seven moons, because when they stumble into the light, he pulls her toward me. Jo's dress is wrinkled. Her slip shows.

"Tell the little fucker," Ray says.

"I'm goin' to St. Louis. With Ray. He's a jet pilot, you know." She pats his arm. He squeezes her like she's a million-dollar prize. "Tell Dad where I am."

They weave through the crowd. At the Tilt-a-Whirl, Josephine looks back and blows me a kiss. I won't see her again, until I don't know when.

* * *

The second thing that happened is that I, too, fell in love.

* * *

Momma would be happy electricity finally came in on singing wires. Dad bought a radio. If Momma were alive, she'd listen to *Arthur Godfrey* and *Queen for A Day,* but I tune in KMOX, to hear Cardinal baseball. I've played ball since I could throw an acorn and root for the Cards when all of Yellowbird gathers at Hord's store to listen to games and hear every word spoken by Harry Caray, the Cardinal's famous announcer.

His descriptions of Stan "The Man" Musial's sweet swing, and Enos "Country" Slaughter's flying cleats, makes me fall into mimic-his-voice-6-4-3 double-play-love. In my mind I play endless imaginary games, broadcasting every pitch, every home run, using my Harry Caray voice, stopping only to cook supper for Dad.

Dad says, "Jeremy, yer momma left a cook book 'round here. Find it. Cookin's good to know. When ya leave home, ya can start a eatin' place and make a good livin'."

I say, "I've looked, but can't find it." Lie's come easy now.

I found the book in a box under the stairs. The first recipe I read called for a pound of finely-chopped beef, a half cup of diced onions, a cup of sifted flour, a half-teaspoon of paprika and cup of wine. We don't have these ingredients and if I ask Dad to buy them, he'd laugh. As it is, I have to beg him to bring home a loaf of bread or dozen eggs.

* * *

Instead of heading off to steal food when Dad leaves for work, I run to my own Sportsman's Park and spend the day with Peanuts Lowery, Red Schoendienst, Cloyd Boyer, Joe Garagiola and other Cardinals. We win every game, beating the New York Giants, Brooklyn Dodgers, Boston Red Sox, Boston Braves or New York Yankees. I pitch, play shortstop or center field, and broadcast every game, every pitch, every home run, using my Harry Caray voice.

One cold day in November, I stop by Lal Hord's store for coal oil. The old men sit around the pot-bellied stove, lying to each other, whittling a whistle for the grand baby or carving faces into their cane. It smells like apples, cattle feed and pipe smoke. I hunker behind a stand of garden seeds, jars of honey and sorghum molasses and pretend I'm Harry Caray, broadcasting an imaginary game.

"Musial, 'The Duke of Denora, Pennsylvania', stands in. His right toe barely touches the ground, weight on his left leg, bat cocked behind his ear, his eyes on Johnny Sain, the Braves All-Star pitcher. Two on. Two out. Sixth inning. Braves lead 4 to 3. Sain winds and pitches. Musial swings. It's a long fly ball. Way, way back there. It might be. It could be. It is! A home run! Holy cow! Stan 'The Man' has put the Cardinals ahead, 6 to 4."

Ol' Man Sam Berry says, "That Musial. Ain't he a cracker jack? Where they playing, Cuba? They'd freeze their balls off 'round here."

Liege Phillips saw me hide. "That weren't no radio, Sam. Hit were that Holt boy. He made ya look dumber a Arkansas hog, neighbor."

The old men laugh and point at Sam. If Josephine were here, she'd giggle. She hated Sam. Once, she told me, "That Old Fool said if I'd come visit him, he'd give me a half dollar. 'Ya pop a maiden 'fore her monthlies, ya got a friend for life,' he said. I'd like to stick a knife in his ribs."

I paid Sam back good, I reckon. When I'm at the door, Mr. Phillips says, "Think that boy sounds like Harry Caray?

Ya oughta hear his fox bark or screech owl call. Best I ever heard."

Somehow, this makes me think of Eddie Zumwalt. Does he still sleep in a dirty room that smells like a privy? When the snow melts, I'll go see him.

* * *

Dad makes me go the church taffy pull with him. His way to meet pretty ladies. Folks are all fired up about the food thief. "Claude Barkley, over by Sunrise School got hit last week. Grab and run. No animal calls. No nothin'." *That wasn't me. Who's stealing my job?*

* * *

The snow melts. Yellow and purple violets sprinkle the creek bottom, and my criminal life calls loud. Boosting dried sausage while a German farmer works his garden fifty feet from his smoke house is more fun than legging out a triple. When Fat Freddie Hubbard, owner of Yellowbird Café, leaves his storeroom door open to carry in eggs and bread, I sneak in and grab a sleeve of Post Toasties boxes and can of potato sticks. That makes the hair on my neck stand up, and I've got snacks for a week.

* * *

The sun hangs in the cedars that circle George Autenrieff's house. He's the old German who makes sausage to sell at Market Day. Around here, Thursday's when the weather's good, farmers bring potatoes, onions, green beans and in season, roasting ears, peaches and watermelons to town to sell or trade, listen to neighbor's talk farming and gossip.

There's no one in the Autenrieff yard that I can see. I crawl to the fence. *Where's that smoke from?* Sausages lay on a rack with fire smoldering beneath them, pale blue smoke wafting up to add favor to fat coils of delicious-smelling pork. I dash to the rack, grab a string of sausages, push them into my bag and dive into the wood pile, crawling fast. George's guineas see me. I'd forgotten about them. With guinea hens, if a blade of grass moves, or a leaf falls from a tree, they'll come running, bodies wobbling like baseballs bouncing over rocks, necks outstretched, squawking to let the world know they've found something wrong. I race to hide behind a log, pulling limbs, wood chips and leaves over me. George yells, "Stella bring my gun. That weasel's back."

When George walks up, the guineas have gone quiet, satisfied to pick at bugs and worms stirred up from the wood chips. I squint to see. He crouches, gun at the ready, a soldier ready to shoot. I smell the manure on his boots. His brown eyes search the wood lot. Then slow, first one foot, then the other, he creeps forward 'til he stands above me. He spits. Tobacco juice bounces off a sapling and splatters onto my nose and cheek. George steps over the log I'm lying behind and settles onto a tree stump.

"Show yerself and die," he whispers. I hope he's talking to the weasel.

The sun beats down on the wood pile. The air is still. My shirt is damp with sweat. My arms itch. I feel pricks on my ankle. A field mouse, eyes bright, wiggles its pink nose and scampers up my leg, pauses at my chest, then on cold feet with sharp nails, races across my neck and disappears. Seconds later, a snake, pink tongue smelling the air, black eyes glistening, emerges between my legs. *What kind is it? A cottonmouth like the one that killed Mom? If I lay real still, it won't bite. Maybe.* I feel cold, rough scales on my bare stomach. It slithers straight for my face. I close my eyes and hold my breathe. My neck feels wet. It crawls across my face to my nose. I see its diamond-shaped head, black tail and white under belly. It's a black snake after a mouse breakfast.

I let air from my lungs slowly. Sweat stings my eyes. My arms feel like spiders walk on them. Needles use my legs for a pin cushion. My nose itches. *Maybe I'll stand. Would George shoot me?*

I'll count. At 1,000 if he's still here, I'll stand, throw my hands over my head and yell, "I give up!"

White clouds sail a blue sky. The sun beats down. I count —"855, 856, 857." George stands, raises one leg, farts and kicks the log above my head.

"I'll set me some traps, Mr. Weasel," he says. "Come back then and yer mine."

He steps over me and walks away, footsteps soft on the grass. At the sausage rack he stops. "S.O.B. got one. Thought my fire would keep varmints away."

Suddenly, I'm so tired I want to sleep. I fill my lungs with air. When I hear the screen door slap shut at the house, I scramble to my feet and run for the creek.

"I seen ya, boy," George hollers. "I seen ya. I'm reportin' ya to the constable." I keep running. *He saw my back. Not my face.* I keep running, the guinea hens squaw, chasing after me. They give up before I reach the grove of pecan trees on the sandy creek bank. I run along the creek, splash to the other side and dive into buck brush. When it seems my heart will stay in my chest after all and my hands stop shaking, I head for my lean-to. *Was one lousy string of sausages worth all that trouble? This is hard work, Holt.*

* * *

Still, on the next Market Day in Yellowbird, I learn a new family has moved into the old Mosely place. They sound like a good target. The husband works for the highway department, so they have money to buy food. I'll do one last raid.

The sun is above the house roof when I belly up to a rick of wood. In the yard, a lady stirs clothes in a kettle of boiling water. *Good. Wash day. I'll hide until she wrings hot water from heavy sheets, then I'll sneak into her kitchen and fill up my sack.*

I lay back and relax. A shadow blocks the sun. My eyes pop open. A young girl's round face almost touches my nose. *Stupid, Holt. You know the rules. Never raid when kids are home. Too unpredictable.*

"Whatcha layin' in the dirt for? Ya'll get cooties."

"Sprained my ankle." I'm good at lying now.

"I'll call Momma." She runs for the lady at the kettle before I can stop her. Her momma comes up, face wet with sweat, dress sleeves pushed to her elbows, damp hair in her eyes.

"Who're you? Whatcha doin' here?"

I stand. "A neighbor, ma'am. Taking a short cut to Yellowbird. Twisted my ankle, so I took a rest." I limp a few steps.

"Yellowbird's the other direction," she says.

"It is? I'm lost, I reckon. I'm new around here. My ankle's fine now."

The little girl says, "If yer lost, turn to Jesus."

Her mother smiles. "Not that kind of lost, dear. What's your name, boy?"

What did I tell the Treadways?

"Stan. Stan Rogers."

"Live 'round here, Stan?"

"Dad and I just moved into the Old Stone place. He's a surveyor. Not home much. Momma died last winter."

"Poor dear. That why you're not in school?"

"Yes, ma'am." Another lie. The truth is, I ditched. If Dad finds out, he'll just yell.

"What's in yer sack?"

"Stuff." I pull out my empty jar. "In case I find a bee tree to rob."

The little girl's blue eyes go wide. "Daddy shoots robbers."

"He's not that kind of robber, dear. Just hungry."

The girl says, "Let Jesus feed him."

"We'll help Jesus," her mother says.

She leads me to her kitchen, fries four eggs, three sausage links and covers it all with gravy. We pray. I eat.

"Stan, are ya washed in the Blood of the Lamb?"

I make my face go serious. "Yes, ma'am."

"Read the Bible?"

"Every day."

"Praise the Lord! Here. Memorize these." She pushes a list of Bible verses toward me.

I shove it into my pocket. When my plate's scraped clean, we pray. Again. At the door, she hands me half an apple pie. "Ya and yer's are welcome at Freewill Baptist any Sunday. Down the road, 'cross the bridge."

The little girl says, "Ya lay in the dirt, ya get cooties."

At the top of the ridge, I look back. The house is a gray shadow beneath blue-green cedars. I wipe tears from my eyes and give out yips like a momma fox calling her kits. *Good haul, Holt. Even if you had to pray.*

* * *

Middle River Creek glistens in the May sun. I cross at a ripple above a good fishing hole. On the other side, the smell of pipe smoke drops me to my knees. Through dried horse weeds I see Liege Phillips and Sam Berry, fishing poles in hand. I crawl downwind to hear them better.

Liege says, “When a family member dies, it bruises the heart. My little brother ain’t been the same since Momma died, forty years come August. Ever bitch dog or mare horse he’s owned, he named Molly. After her.”

Sam nods. “That Holt boy has plain gone nuts since his momma died. Saturday night I turned my black and lemon-spotted gyp loose for the race.” What did Josephine say about Sam? *He eats gooseberries, his face is so sour.*

Sam’s talking fox hunting. Most Saturday nights, hunters turn their dogs loose in Dad’s stand of timber in the creek bottom. There’s more than one fox den there.

Sam says, “She were ‘bout to come in heat, but figured to get one last race ‘fore I bred her. Fox holed up after three, four hours, but my little girl didn’t come in. Went lookin’ Sunday mornin’. Stopped by the Holt place. That boy were runnin’ ‘round, blabbin’ like a edjit. I hallooed. He never answered. Boy’s plumb crazy.”

Liege shakes his head. “Mebbe. Might been playin’. His daddy gone a lot lookin’ fer hair pie. Boy needs somethin’ to pass the time.”

“Could be. Still, ya said yerself he’s right good at animal calls. Don’t that food stealin’ sonofabitch make a fox bark or turkey gobble after he stole something? I suspicion that Holt boy’s the guilty one. Told Constable Mike Chambers so when I seen him last week.”

Liege spits out his chaw. “Ya did, did ya? Ain’t ya the smart one. I figger our thief’s a grown man. Strikes, night or day. That boy's in school, most days. 'Sides, I hear he cooks good as a woman." I smile. *Josephine, would love to know I'm a good cook.*

Liege says, "They ever hear from the daughter? Th' blonde that Maxie boy followed off somewhere's?"

"No. Don't expect they care to, neither. Her bein' a slut and all."

Not true, Sam. I miss Josephine. So does Dad. She's not a slut. Whatever that is.

Sam says, "My cellar's chockful. That food thief edjit comes to steal my stuff, young or old, he gets a taste of buckshot. Double ought. In the gut."

That does it. Sam Berry, I'm gonna rob your ass.

* * *

It's a bad year for my Cardinals. By July of '51, they'll have to get hot and stay that way to finish in first division. Yellowbird celebrates the 4th with fire crackers, Roman candles and baseball. In the men's game, the Yellowbird Jays beat the Mokane Bulldogs. My team, the Junior Jays, play next.

Dad promised to watch. I search sun-burned faces behind home plate. No Dad. *A widow must need her porch swing adjusted. That'll take him all day. Maybe two.*

We win our game big. I got three hits, drove in four runs and struck out twelve. When Dad comes home two days later, he doesn't ask how the ball game went. He says, "Grab a scythe, Jeremy, and cut them weeds down by the mailbox. People'll think we're trash, lettin' weeds grow wild."

I do as he say, but I'm frosted. He treats me worse than Eddie Zumwalt's folks treat him, except now that Corrie

Ann Pannell does our laundry, my sheets are cleaner. I miss Momma and the cinnamon toast she'd fix me Sunday mornings, and how she'd dance a jig and kiss my forehead when I'd recite the times tables through fifteen.

* * *

Monday morning, the Twelfth of July, breaks hot and clear. Every crow caw from the walnut trees down by the fence, every grasshopper that flits from weed-to-weed on my ball park grass, every meadowlark call makes me pine for my thieving days. Even an important three game series, the Cards against Ewell Blackwell and the Cincinnati Reds, loses its shine.

When the sun is high enough I can step on my own shadow, I toss my glove in the dugout, grab my sack and trot over to Sam Berry's house. It's time he paid for calling Josephine a name. He said his pantry was filled, and brags all the time his wife, Myrna, grows a great garden. It should be a good raid that gives me food for two weeks.

I lay in the weeds and plan my attack. Sam doesn't drive, so there's no car or truck to worry about. The back-porch light is on; the house quiet. Sam must be in the field with his mules, since the corral behind his wood lot is deserted.

His cellar is my target. I scamper to the apple tree next to the well and hide. The female foxhound Sam spoke of at the creek back in May, is tied by the smoke house. I flip a rock at her. She raises her head, sniffs and lays back down. *She has a swollen belly and breathes fast. Is she about to have pups?*

I run to the lilac bush, wait a minute, then race to the cellar, open the door and roll inside.The air is black and cool. When my eyes adjust to the light, I search every shelf, looking for green beans, sauerkraut, tomatoes, blackberry jam, food most every cellar has. Sam's shelves are bare. Even the apple barrel beside the door is empty. *What the hell, Sam? Where's all that grub you bragged about?*

Outside, squinting against the bright sun, I hide behind the wood pile to see if anyone comes out of the house. When no one does, I race to the road ditch, dive in among cow cabbage and horse weeds, wiggle through the culvert, push through tall mullein, and keep in the ditch past the pasture, to where the road curves. *I'm flabbergasted. Sam's cellar was empty as a post hole.*

Dad says an empty barrel makes more noise than a full one. Momma said, "Those that have, have. Those who don't, brag."

* * *

A couple of weeks later after playing imaginary ball all morning, I'm starved. Dad's been gone for two days. Last fall I hid a jar of dried beef, a quart of carrots, and canned peaches at my hideout near Rabbit's Gap. If I take the short cut over Cedar Creek Bridge, I can get there, eat, and run home before the Cardinal's game is over. Musial loves to hit against the Reds. *I wonder if Dad'll come home tonight?*

I half walk, half trot beneath ash and sycamore trees that line the newly-graveled road.This side of the Cedar Creek Bridge, a black Chevrolet is parked in the shade. Constable Mike Chambers sits on the fender.

"Don't limp much for a kid with a sprained ankle," He says. He stands and stretches.

I'm taken aback. How does he know I told that nice lady over by Freewill Baptist I'd sprained my ankle? Won't you ever learn Holt? Keep your mouth shut.

The constable is tall with blue eyes.

I say, "Nothing wrong with me."

Constable Chambers' tan shirt and tan trousers are starched and ironed. His black boots shine. He wears a white cowboy hat. A pistol gleams in black leather holster.

Does Corrie Ann Pannell do his laundry, too?

"A lady I know says you sprained an ankle. What's in the sack?"

"Nothing." My hands shake. I pull out my jar. "For grasshoppers. Or worms. I fish some."

"That all?"

"No, sir. For water." I wave a blue enamel cup. "A paper sack for mushrooms or fallen fruit." I'm breathing fast, too.

The constable says, "I knew your mom. She was a good woman."

"Thank you, sir."

Chambers puts his hat on the car roof. When he umpires ball games he wears a blue shirt and black pants. Dad said Chambers was too old to be a soldier during the war, so he worked at a defense plant in St. Louis. When the war ended, he and his wife moved back to Yellowbird. Dad thinks he'll run for sheriff.

"Been over by Freewill Baptist lately?"

"Had a trot line in the creek there for a while." If he asks how many hooks, I'm a goner. I lied. I don't fish. Momma said the truth will out.

"Know a kid named Stan Rogers?"

"Nope." That's no lie. That was the name I used at the Treadway's and with the lady who cooked me breakfast. Constable asked did I know Stan, not was I Stan.

"You and your daddy move?"

"No, sir."

"This Stan kid told this lady he and his Daddy moved into the old Stone place. Described you to a tee."

"The Stone place? That farm just west of the iron bridge? That the Zumwalt's own? Dad said he'd stop by there and ask if they needed any work done."

"He do any?"

"Don't know. He only tells me to get supper on the table."

The constable laughs. He puts on his hat and taps it in place. "Stopped by there. It's abandoned." His foot on the running board, he says, "Stan, whose stealing food from folks 'round here?"

"Name's Jeremy." *Did he call me "Stan" on purpose?*

Chambers ignores this. "Miss Alice said Stan brought her goods from a grocery truck wreck. Know anything about that?"

"Nope."

"Me neither. That the Treadway's got free grub is not my concern. Givin' old folks food is no crime, if no money's involved. Crooks sell what they steal. I cataloged what was left of the Treadway's haul. Labels tell me it was store bought." He adjusts his wide belt.

"What's puzzles me is the food that's boasted from folk's pantry or cellar. Some say they hear animal calls and when they look the food's gone. Others hear nothing. Two different perps the way, I see it. Probably hoboes. You get around. See any strangers?"

He hasn't mention the German sausages that I stole. He must not know about them. Now's my chance to lie. "I'm not sure, but last week a limb line that usually catches fish was empty. It was baited differently from how I bait. I saw a camp fire's ashes in the woods."

"Good looking out. Keep your eyes peeled. See anything suspicious, have your Dad contact me." He opens his car door.

"The Treadway's Good Samaritan had a truck or wagon to move all that grub. Your momma's folks used a travois. She teach you to make one?"

"Yes sir."

I add, "The Zumwalt's own the old Stone place. You talk to them?" *If he goes by their house, maybe he'll find Eddie and forget about me.*

"Not yet. But I will." He slides into his car. "Thanks for the intel." He rolls down his car window. "I figure this Stan kid doesn't have a momma. Steals to eat. You see him, tell him what he's nabbed up to now is only a misdemeanor. He'd get no jail time. Nothing on his record. If he stops, so does my investigation."

His car motor jolts to life. "You've got a future as a ball player, Jeremy. You get arrested, no big-league club will give you a chance." He smiles. "I'm going right past the cut off to Rabbit's Gap. Give you a lift?"

How'd he know that's where I'm headed?

"No, thanks. Have to check my limb lines."

"Suit yourself. My next day off, maybe I'll stop by. We'll drown some worms, okay?"

"Sure." That would mean trouble for me. I don't have a favorite fishing hole.

"Think I oughta stop by the Zumwalt's, huh?" He leans out the window. "We'll talk again. Remember, I always get my man."

I just nod.

* * *

At my camp, I open the peaches. *Constable Chambers thinks I'm the food thief. I shouldn't have mentioned the Zumwalt's. If he learns their pantry was raided, he'll compare what they lost with the list he made at Treadway's. Then he'll come arrest me.*

My gut growls. *If I start a fire, Chambers might see the smoke. He'll figure it's me and come for a look see. It's peaches and spring water, Holt.*

I fill my bottle. The valley stretches south to Yellowbird. A gentle wind moves the trees. Clouds make dark shadows on the green grass. Crows rise like black smoke against the blue sky, their caws loud.

They're spooked.

I scan the hillside. *Why would someone put a single fence post in a pasture? It's not a post, it moves. The Constable! If he catches me with food, it'll be jail time for me.*

I hide the jars behind rocks in the cave. *Where can I hide? The cave? No. He'll see my foot prints. A hickory tree. Maybe.*

My intruder on the hillside goes left at the fork like he's going to our house. *Does Chambers know this area that well? Something about the way this person walks is familiar. Is it a girl?*

The sun comes from behind a cloud, and the walker's head catches fire. *Only one person in the world has hair that bright and shiny. Josephine!*

In *Wind In the Willows* when Toad came home, there was a big celebration. "Bang! go the drums! The trumpeters are tooting and the soldiers are saluting, and the cannon they are shooting and the motor-cars are hooting, as the – Hero – comes!"

I run to get the canned carrots and dried beef from the

cave, since Jo and I will need eats. Then I trot down the path to meet her, ready to toot and salute and shoot.

* * *

Jo sits on a rock beneath a walnut tree when I come up. “You lost,” I ask, handing her my water bottle.

She drinks. “Just tired, Jeremy. Take me home.”

“How’d ya get here?”

“Bus to Jeff City. The Weekly to Yellowbird. Walked from there. Think Daddy’ll let me stay?”

“Dunno. He was mad you left.”

“He was? You told him where I went, right?”

“Yeah. He slapped me. Said I shouldn’t have let you go.”

“He did?”

“Yeah. Said he had a rat he thought your cooking could kill.”

She doesn’t laugh. “He still mad?”

“He’ll get over it. Maybe.”

“My suitcase is at the stile.”

“I’ll fetch it tomorrow.”

Josephine leans against me as we limp home like base runners blocked off home plate by a catcher in shin guards. There Jo lays on the divan. I rustle up supper. Yesterday, I boiled some beets. I add the carrots from my sack to them. In another pan, I stir evaporated milk into the beef, drop in chopped tomatoes, onions and a chunk of oleo and let it simmer. *If Dad’s home, I bet he’ll like this.*

The moon floats in the eastern sky when, surprise, Dad pulls into the yard. He stops for a slug of bourbon in the tool shed, washes up on the back porch, comes into the kitchen and sits. He sees Josephine, but doesn't speak, just eats. Jo's moist eyes study her fork and spoon. Dad sops bread in beef gravy, swallows and pushes his coffee cup toward me. I refill it.

He takes a sip and turns to Jo. "Ya came home, huh? Yer bed's upstairs. Help Jeremy in the kitchen. Don't run off agin, hear."

* * *

Josephine would sleep all day if Dad didn't rouse her out before he leaves for work mornings. She sits on the back porch, fingering her necklace, as shadows grow long, then short and long again. Once, she held the necklace for me to see. "Real rubies."

"Where'd you get 'em?"

"A gentleman friend."

* * *

Before St. Louis, if Josephine wanted a *Photoplay Magazine* she'd count out the exact change, money she'd saved from what Dad gave her for Market Day. "Hide it down by the creek."

Now, she pulls a dollar from her pocketbook, wads it up and tosses it to me. "Bring me a *True Confessions and Modern Screen.* Pack of Luckys. Keep the change."

"I'm not old enough to buy cigarettes."

"Put your money on the counter. You'll get 'em."

She's right. I buy fags without questions. Sometimes, I spend a nickel on a Grapette or Fudgesicle, but usually I drop the change in a work glove hanging in the chicken house. I want a real bat, not the peeled persimmon sprout I use now.

"Hide your magazines?"

"Hell, no. I'm old enough to read what I want." She'll turn fifteen, November 10th.

She picks up the cigarette pack. "Know what L.S.M.F.T. stands for?"

I listen to the radio. "Lucky Strike Means Fine Tobacco."

She laughs. "Loose Strap Means Floppy Tits." My eyes go big. She says, "Grow up, Little Brother."

* * *

I come home from school. Jo's asleep on the divan. I shake her awake. We take PB and J sandwiches outside. The breeze carries a meadow lark's call. Josephine wears a white slip and red brassiere, blonde hair knotted at her neck, her freckles brown as last year's oak leaves.

"All this quiet gives me the creeps." She shivers and puffs on her Lucky. "A funny thing happened one night at the tourist court where Ray and I stayed. He woke up, crying. Said he didn't know how to get in a jet, much less fly one. Said the car we were driving was one he stole, and he misses his momma. He commenced to boohoo saying the pickle we were in was my fault 'cause I didn't ask where he got the car or how we could live with no one working. I shushed him back to sleep, tied him to the bed with his phony necktie and called the cops from a pay phone across the street. Told 'em where to find a car thief, then took a taxi downtown."

I nod.

"I aimed to catch a Greyhound home, but the Mid-American Theatre had a double feature. I couldn't miss Ilene Woods in *Cinderella.* And you know how I love Liz Taylor.

A Place in the Sun, was the feature film. That Monty Clift. What a dream boat! I watched both shows twice, then went to the john. A lady offered to buy me coffee and a hotdog. Said if I was older, she had a job for me. I said, 'I'm eighteen.' I worked that night."

"What 'ya do?"

"Look pretty and wiggle."

* * *

Saturday night, Dad comes home early. "You went to school with that Zumwalt boy, right? The one with the shakes? Eddie?"

"Yeah."

I act like this is of no interest to me. *I was stupid to suggest that Constable Chambers visit them.*

"Mike Chambers found him locked in a room dirty as a hog sty. Boy covered in filth. Chambers had him cleaned up, then went by the Blue Moon and told Eddie's folks to take better care of their son or go to jail. They found a place in Jeff City that handles his kind."

"Good for them," Jo says.

"Good for the constable," I say.

"Chambers was at the post office. Said to tell you he'll be by to go fishin'. I said ya don't fish. He said he didn't think you did, but you'll be a damn good poker player someday. Think he meant ball player?"

* * *

Sunday afternoon, two weeks or so later, Dad busts into the house waving an envelope. "We gotta shake a leg," he says. "Bertha Sawyer an' her edjit stepson are due any minute. Letter in the mail box. Says they're comin' early afternoon."

This was before we had two telephones that rang all

the time and worked day and night running a dairy. Dad yells upstairs to Josephine. “Yer suitor’s comin’. Get dressed.”

Josephine comes down the steps fast, like she’s trying to beat out a bunt. “What suitor?”

“Read it yerself.” He hands her the letter. “Says Curt Sawyer’s comin’to declare his intentions regardin’ my daughter.” Dad laughs. “Sounds like weddin’ bells are gonna chime.” He has a catcher’s build, wide shoulders, long arms, big hands.

Josephine says, “Curt? He’s dumb as creek rock. We talked at school. Once. Bought me a Cocola. Told me how he plants corn.”

“Ya musta impressed him. Beats hell outta runnin’ off to St. Louis with a Army boy you met at a carnival, don’t it?”

“Air Force,” Josephine says. “He said Air Force.”

Dad ignores this. “Put on a clean dress. Brush yer hair.”

“I’m tired. Change of climate I guess, and . . .and other things.” She’s tuning up to cry.

“Dry up, dammit. Yer beau’s comin’.”

Dad turns to me. “Jeremy, any strawberry jam left?”

“No, sir. Just Karo Syrup.”

Corrie Ann Pannell’s kids cleaned out our tomatoes and cucumbers last week and Dad hasn’t bought groceries in a month. The rest of our garden went to waste with no one to can vegetables.

“Breakfast biscuits?”

“Two.”

“Split ‘em. Heat ‘em up. Fix yer peanut butter and Karo syrup concoction. Set a table. Knives. Saucers. No chips. Use them napkins in yer Momma’s cedar chest.”

I groan.

"Soon as they're settled in, you can play. Love birds get the front room. I'll entertain Mrs. Sawyer."

I've just put the last saucer on the table when a Model "A" Ford pulls into the front yard. Curt Sawyer and his step-mom climb out. Curt's tall as a first baseman. He wears a flat top straw hat, white shirt, blue-striped tie, black britches and brown shoes.

I figured Mrs. Sawyer to be umpire ugly, but she wears a pink and white checked suit with round silver buttons down the front and a white ruffle at her throat. Her hair's black as Ava Gardner's.

"I hope you got my letter." She shakes Dad's hand. "This is a surprise to me, too."

Dad says, "Come in. Come in."

Curt stares at Josephine, his face red as a batter who struck out with the bases loaded. He tries to take her hand. Her right hand twists her necklace.

Dad says to Mrs. Sawyer, "My daughter, Josephine. Answers to Jo. My boy, Jeremy."

I say, "May I offer you some tea, or do you prefer water?"

"What delightful manners, Jeremy."

I nod. If you have a lady's upside-down pineapple cake in your sack and your sack is under her porch and you're on all fours in her flower bed next to her house and she asks if you've seen any strangers, it's best to be polite. Removes suspicion. Same thing now.

"Tea, please. Two sugars. Curt, what would you like, dear?"

"Whatever Josephine's havin'."

His collar is wet from sweat. He eyes Jo like she's a chicken leg and he hasn't eaten for days. I bring the drinks.

Dad says, “When my Victrola broke, I never got it fixed. Bought a Philco when electricity came through.” It plays church music now.

Mrs. Sawyer nods. “That was smart, Buller. When Curt’s daddy passed, I had the lazyies for a year or more. Poor Curt had to fend for himself. His father and I had no children of our own. Curt’s my only family.”

Baseball calls me. I back out the door. The regular season ended when the Yankees beat the Giants in the World Series, 4 games to 2, but for me, it’s always time for baseball. I start for my diamond, when I remember my ball glove was dew-soaked this morning. I hung it outside the front room window to dry. It’ll need oiling.

* * *

Around front, I pour neatsfoot oil into my glove and rub it in. The window’s wide open. Curt sits on the divan. I could touch him if I want. Josephine’s in a chair by the door.

Curt says, “It don’t bother me none what you done in St. Louis, nor what folks say you did. I can’t swallow or even breathe when you cross my mind. Which is mostly all the time. Daddy left me eighty-four acres with a fine house and good out buildin’s. We could make a go, me and you. I’d be more‘n proud to carry you to Jeff City Saturdays for a picture show and ice cream at Central Dairy.”

“I’m not the farmer’s wife type,” Jo says. “Don’t know how to garden. Can vegetables. Butcher hogs.”

“You’d learn. Or we’d hire it out.”

“We’d hate each other in six months.”

“I’d never hate you.”

“You’re nice, but I’ll pass. You’ll find the right girl

someday."

"Don't want nobody else 'cept you."

Jo's voice is clear as Hy Everback, the radio announcer. "I'd rather African ants ate me alive than marry you." She's out the door.

Curt stumbles outside and runs to find Bertha, in the front yard. "She wants to think on it," he blubbers.

Bertha says, "When a young lady wishes to think on a marriage proposal, she means no."

"I'll die if she don't marry me."

"Shush," Bertha says. "You think you will. But you won't. Go sit in the car while Mr. Holt and I finish our business."

She goes to the porch where Dad is. He hands her an arm load of lilacs. "How thoughtful, Buller. My troubles vanish when I'm with you."

Around back, Josephine asks, "Hear any of that?"

"Any of what?"

"Curt's bullshit?"

I shake no. She carries her tea glass. "Where does Daddy hide his whiskey?"

I shrug.

"Don't give me that crap. Where?"

"If I was looking I'd try the tool shed. Second beam over."

She hands me her glass. "Three fingers. If he sees me there, he might figure out what I'm after." I don't tell her Dad's on the front porch giving lilacs to Mrs. Sawyer.

In the shed, I dump a slug of Hill and Hill into Josephine's glass and bring it to her. She gulps it down. "Men are so dumb. Present company excluded."

* * *

In my game, Harry Caray is in the broadcast booth. "Two balls and one strike on Sam Jethro. He joined the Braves from the Negro League. Howie Pollet winds and fires. Jethro swings. It's a long fly ball to center field. Holt goes back, back. He leaps, crashes into the wall, falls to the grass, but holds onto the ball. Holy cow! What a catch! Third out. Cards lead Boston 3 to 2. Bottom of the eighth coming up."

I jump up and trot past Dad and Mrs. Sawyer. She says, "Buller, with two springs, a nice pond and good pasture you could handle what, forty cows?"

"'Spect so. Maybe fifty.

"Dairy products sell like nylons these days. You could have yourself a fine dairy here.

"Where'd I get money for cows?"

"What about that stand of timber you mentioned?"

"Why didn't I think of that?"

Bertha touches his arm. "Buller Holt, you're such a tease. You've already figured your profit, smart as you are."

* * *

Wednesday after Mrs. Sawyer and Curt's visit, the sky streaks red, green and blue when Dad parks his truck under the big elm. He smells like Brilliantine and witch-hazel. He swallows supper, pushes his chair back and says, "Me and Bertha's getting' married. Startin' a dairy. Her dead husband left her a few bucks. I'll sell timber for my share. Thirty Holsteins and five milkin' machines at first."

What does he mean? Will he tear down my Sportsman Park? Will Mrs. Sawyer be my momma? Will she live with us, or us with her? Will Curt be Josephine's brother? Can love birds marry kin?

Dad taps my arm. "Go outside. Me and Josephine wanna talk."

I run to the yard, circle the privy and come up on the screened-in porch side of the house. I stand next to a cherry tree and hear every word they say.

Josephine says, "Hurryin' things, aren't you?"

"Givin' the lady her wish." He pours coffee. "Bertha wants ya to marry Curt. He'll do deliveries for the dairy. Ain't right him relivin' his failure ever time he sees ya. Here's the deal. Marry him or move out. He ain't ideal, but what man is?"

Jo says, "I wouldn't marry that sorry son-of-a-bitch if I got Montgomery Cliff as boot, and Frank Sinatra sang *Indian Love Song* at the ceremony." She goes to the stove. "Know why I sleep so much? I just . . ."

"Girl's do that at their time of month, Bertha says."

"Bertha don't know shit."

"That's my future wife and yer stepmother yer slan-derin'. Knock it off."

Jo twists her necklace. "I can't believe you'd want me to hook up that turd, Curt. I'll leave tomorrow."

The weekly runs Thursdays.

Dad says, "Ya oughta be thankful he'd have ya. Tar-nished like ya are."

"I'm too good for his silly ass. He's so dumb he'd eat a frog raw if I told him to. I'm gone." She climbs the stairs two at a time.

Dad comes into the yard. He sees me at the porch but says nothing. "Jeremy, stop playin' them make-believe ball games. Bertha's 'fraid you'll confuse the difference 'tween real and make believe. Knock 'em off, hear?"

I nod. Bertha's an umpire, after all.

* * *

Two days later, Dad comes home, washes up on the back porch and in a hurry, changes into tan britches, clean socks and Sunday shoes. I pile his dirty clothes on the back porch for Corrie Ann Pannell.

"I'll spend the night in town. Tomorrow, when you get home from school, start gettin' the garden ready for fall plantin'. No imaginary ball playin', hear.

He doesn't call upstairs to Josephine, just drives off. His headlights disappear down by the creek, then, like a fire fly, wink uphill and fade into the night.

Josephine comes downstairs. "Got your marching orders, huh?" Her face is white as a sliced onion. "Get Daddy's whiskey. I need a shot."

I have questions, but who do I ask? I run for the bottle.

Josephine knocks back a swig then pours some into a glass and adds water. She sits on her legs, the kitchen light at her back, her arms wrapped in her dress. "You're an uncle. Or were anyway." Tears spill down her cheeks.

Like a radio with static, some of her words are clear, others garbled. "I was so dumb. I'd eat a big supper and still be hungry. Packed on the pounds. One morning my belly hurt something awful. Thought I had to puke, but nothing came up."

She doesn't look at me, she looks toward me. She may be here on the well while whippoor-wills call and tree frogs peep and a quarter moon floats in a starry sky, but she's really somewhere far, far away.

* * *

What's wrong with me, the young girl wonders. *Did I eat bad food?*

Pain shoots through her abdomen and legs as she creeps down the hall to the bathroom, her blonde hair dark from sweat. She sits, but only passes gas. She staggers back to her room, crawls into bed and sobs into her pillow.

Bridgette, from the next room over, pokes her head in. "Got a problem, Blondie?"

"Sick. Ache all over."

"You havin' a baby?"

The young girl opens her eyes wide, but pain closes her throat. Bridgette comes closer."Occupational hazard. This ain't no place for a baby. Got any money?"

The girl thinks, what a stupid question. "Why?"

"For a doctor."

"Nine bucks." She doesn't mention the match box stuffed with folded bills in her drawer, or the twenty sewed into the lining of her pocket book, tricks a former roommate taught her. Three young ladies in slips and bras, frazzled hair and wide eyes, crowd into the room. Bridgette says, "I know where you can go, Blondie. No cost. Okay?"

The young girl nods. Bridgette disappears. Coins rattle in a pay telephone. The young girl senses something bad is happening, but the pain makes it hard to think.

From the foot of her bed, the girl with red hair and white face says, "I've had two kids. First one's hardest."

Bridgette comes back. She throws a dress at the young girl. "Put this on. We'll slip out the back stairs."

The young girl has seen Boss Wanda cuss and slap girls when they're sick and can't work. She doesn't want that. She stands. The bed whirls. Her mouth tastes sour. She buttons the dress, pins on her hat, stuffs clean underwear and the matchbox into a sack, grabs her pocketbook, creeps downstairs and out the side door. They wait under a peach tree, two alleys over. A beat-up Plymouth pulls up. The driver hands Bridgette an envelope.

"Thanks for 'memberin' us."

Bridgette pushes the young girl into the car. "You're on your own, Sister."

* * *

The driver gives her a long look. He wears a white shirt, a sweat-stained straw hat and needs a shave. The car smells like cat piss. "Got into trouble, huh? Ya still look good."

He tosses her a scratchy blanket. "Cover up with this. Ain't nobody's business but our'n what we's up to."

Under the blanket, the girl closes her eyes, but pain keeps her awake. She manages a quick glance out the window. Corn stalks and trees whiz by. Her body aches. She drowses until someone screams.

"Knock that shit off, gal," the driver yells.

The car keeps going and going. The girl's blanket is wet. Her head aches. Her lips are chapped. Her mouth dry. After what seems like hours the car jolts to a stop in front of a two-story white house with green shutters. A black lady comes to the car. "This yo' first one, honey?"

The young girl says, "I'm having a baby." She's embarrassed, yet proud. *Why didn't I know sooner?*

"Ya sure are," the Negress says. She leads the young girl to a small cot in a small room. When she lays down, the pain hits again. Hard. The young girl cries, "I'm sorry, Daddy. I'm sorry."

She drowses on a mattress. *What doesn't someone help me?* The room fills with shadows. A woman hurries by. The young girl tries to wave, but her arms are tied. "I'm having a baby," she calls. *What's wrong with people? Can't they see I need help?* She falls asleep. When she wakes her insides are on fire.

The Negro lady stands over her. "Push, chile, push."

The young girl feels something somewhere move. A voice says, "It's a fine baby boy."

A doll the size of Jeremy's ball glove is on her stomach, red skin wrinkled, arms beating the air. The young girl reaches for him. To hold him. Kiss him. Straps pin her arms to her side. She watches as another lady wraps her baby in a pink blanket and carries him away, never to see her son again.

* * *

Like a base runner tagged out on the hidden ball trick, Josephine shakes her head to clear the fog. She seems surprised to see she's sitting on the well beneath a tall maple at home.

"I don't know where they took him or why," she whispers. "That's why I sleep so much. I had a baby. He was stolen. Nobody gives a shit."

I put my arms around her. She pushes me away, grabs the whiskey bottle and chugs, her face red. After a minute, she says, "Help me upstairs, Jeremy."

* * *

Dad's bed yawns empty when my feet hit the cold linoleum floor. I'd like to sleep, but it's a school day. Then, I remember Josephine. I dress, run to the apple tree and fill my overall bib with windfalls. Back in the kitchen, I slice one, sprinkle on cinnamon and take it up to Jo. She won't answer the door. I set the plate down and run to Sportsman's Park, where the Cards play the Yankees.

Think I'll play a double header. How will Dad know? When the sun hits the pitcher's mound, I pretend my game has a rain delay and go up to the house.

There's a heel of bread in the pantry along with a can of hominy, tin of Spam and the apples I picked earlier. I scrape mold off the bread, smear on the last of the butter, shake on sugar and add cinnamon. When the oven's hot, the bread goes on an upside-down pie pan on the top shelf. The toast bubbles golden brown, I take it up to Jo. She smiles when I come in.

She wears a black brassiere and pink slip. She dabs perfume behind her ear. Blond hair frames her white face. She crushes her cigarette in a saucer and sits on the bed, legs crossed at the ankle. Red-tipped fingers lift brown toast to scarlet lips.

"Gonna walk me to Yellowbird? Or play ball like you're not supposed to?"

"Play ball, I guess."

"I thought so. Ya tell Daddy what I told ya?"

"Nope." She doesn't know he didn't come home.

Jo pulls on a yellow dress, ties brown shoe laces and picks up her straw suitcase. On the porch, she kisses my cheek. "Take care, Little Brother."

* * *

My throat hurts. My eyes are wet. I run to the ball diamond, but the thrill of playing center field between Musial and Slaughter is gone. My persimmon bat feels silly. I remember the work glove in the chicken house and the money I saved for a new bat. I run and grab the glove. *It's three miles to Yellowbird. If I hustle maybe I'll get there before the Weekly leaves.*

I race past oak trees and under hickories, through knee-high alfalfa like I'm chasing fly balls in the real Sportsman's Park. The bus is about to pull away when I run up. Josephine sticks her head out a window. I hand her the glove. Our fingers touch as the bus chugs off.

"Buy yourself a *Photoplay* or pack of gum," I yell.

"Thanks. You're a better man than our daddy." She blows me a kiss.

* * *

When the bus disappears around the bend, I run home. There are yams to dig and snap pea vines to pull and dirt to ready for kale and winter cabbage. I try to force my shovel into the ground, but I'm weak as Josephine the day she came home from St. Louis. I fall in a heap on warm dirt.

"Thief, thief," yanks me awake. *Constable Chambers is putting handcuffs on me.* I sit up. A blue jay dips into the cedar tree.

I could drink a creek dry. At the well, the smell of Jo's cigarette smoke and perfume makes my jaws ache. The wind moans in the maple like a baby crying.

* * *

Two weeks later, Bertha moves in. Dad's new wife. The work to turn our farm into a dairy begins with a new fence and gate. The barn floor is levelled, concrete poured. Water tanks, stanchions and milking machines are installed. Then the cows arrive. Twenty black and white Holsteins to be milked twice a day, every day, their milk processed and taken to the Co-op. A guy with a truck piles dirt in a big mound in the middle of the barn yard for the cows to stand on. That's supposed to make them happy.

Things change in the house, too. Dad and Bertha move into Josephine's room upstairs. Curt's bed is where Momma's once was. He plays his radio all night. "Helps me sleep," he says when Dad tells him to knock it off. "Keeps everone else awake," Dad says.

"Now, Buller. You handle the dairy. I'll handle Curt. If he listens to his radio at night it's a small inconvenience."

Dad rolls his eyes and stomps out.

* * *

Since Bertha was a school teacher, the Yellowbird school board lets her give me lessons at home, so I'll have more time to work. A proctor comes every two weeks to see I don't cheat on my exams. Most days I shovel cow manure, hose down heifers, wash milk cans, load ten-gallon cans of milk onto Curt's truck and do a million other chores. The dairy business is work, work, work. Twenty-four hours a day, seven days a week.

So I can stack hay, dig ditches, and shovel corn, Bertha asks the school board to let me take all required tests to complete the eighth grade in a week. They agree. My schooling ends before Thanksgiving.

I wish Josephine was here to see the Old Homestead. She wouldn't get the creeps from the silence now. Cows moo, milk cans bang, electric motors hum, men yell, and always, the bang of hammers. This fall, Bertha had Momma's roses along the front fence yanked out and lilacs planted, dark sticks in the ground. *I wonder how Momma felt seeing her roses thrown away?*

The barn yard is thick mud, deep and black like rotten

leaves under an elm tree. Thick and gooey it mixes with cow manure and pulls at boots, covers pant legs, splashes in your face, and plasters your hair down. Two showers a day in the milk testing room leave me feeling gritty and grimy. And everywhere the smell of warm milk, bleach and sun baking cow manure.

I haven't heard one whit from Josephine. Most evenings when the first star winks in the sky, I make a wish, but she hasn't shown yet.

* * *

Bertha's right. Dairy products do sell fast. The post-War economy, the experts call it. Curt works hard to deliver milk to the co-op and grocery stores. "Momma said the best way to get over one girl is get another one. I ask ever girl I see for a date. Like Josephine, they all say no." On my fourteenth birthday, I get a driver's license that allows me to drive a farm vehicle.

"Now ya can do real work," Dad says. He buys a used ¾ ton truck, has a red and white sign painted on the door that says, Blue Sky Dairy. "Be sure ya get paid for ever quart of milk. and egg you deliver to them college boys and gals in Columbia. We ain't runnin' a charity, ya know." He sways back and forth as talks. "Ya wreck this truck, I'll wreck ya."

One day Corrie Ann Pannell visits. When she leaves, her cousin, Milred, is our cook. Her two sons, Luke and John, hire on to run the milk separator, wash cans and operate the bottler. Milred cooks for 8, three times a day, each eating at a different time. Curt and his mail-order wife, Gretchen, eat early mornings, then late afternoon and early evening. Jaybird Brandenburg, (we hired him in October of '55,) eats after morning and after evening milking. Dad and Bertha have a meal whenever they want. Luke and John and I usually eat mornings and late afternoon.

Milred has a yellow complexion, with brown freckles across her nose, her hair tied up with a nylon hose, floppy slippers on her long feet. She fries great chicken and bakes fluffy biscuits. Yes, Josephine, my dear, things are different around the old farm now a days.

Dad wanders in sometimes when I'm eating, yelling for me to do this chore or that. I just smile and tear into Milred's meat loaf or ham hock and Navy beans. Dad must miss his trips to the Post Office to see the ladies, or breakfast at the Yellowbird Café. If he does get free, Bertha goes with him, and they're back in a hurry. Mostly, Dad putters around adjusting stanchions, testing regulators, repairing busted barn doors. He slips down to the creek for a nip of bourbon two or three times a day.

Bertha's at her station every morning. Winter time, it's the back porch, an electric blanket over her shoulders, lipstick and makeup on like she's going to church, wearing a mink coat and fur-trimmed overshoes, a red bandana tied around her black hair, her account ledger near at hand. Summers, her throne is the bottling plant.

If something goes wrong she can't handle, she'll call, "Jeremy dear. Go straighten up that mess will you, please?" Sweet words in a brittle voice.

I seldom think about Constable Chamber. He ran for sheriff as Dad predicted, but tailed the ticket, so he bought a farm over by Auxvasse, and started a catfish farm. I don't have time to steal a four-leaf clover, much less a peach cobbler from a newly-married bride.

I haven't heard anyone talk about the Food Thief for years, except Jay Bird. One day as he was pocketing his pay check, he thanked Bertha, then turned to me. “Ya been friend to my family for years. Hell, that grub ya got from that grocery truck wreck fed us for a month.”

“That wasn’t me. That was Stan Rogers.”

“Ya two sure look alike.”

“So, I’ve been told.”

* * *

The Cardinals make a run for the pennant in 1953, ’54, and ’56, but not even Stan “The Man” can hold off the Giants and the Dodgers. April, our third year in operation carpenters add two rooms to the house. Bertha moves to the old front room, so “Your Dad can have his privacy upstairs.” Curt’s mail order bride arrived in June. “They’s weddin’ boudoir is next to his Momma’s room,” Dad laughs. “They won’t be rumblin’ sheets with her ear to the door.”

In June 1957, almost five years since the dairy started operations and two days before my nineteenth birthday, I grab some eggs and coffee after changing a flat tire on the truck. As I go back outside, Bertha’s trash can is in the hall.

I’m going by the burn barrel, so I grab the can. When I dump it, a puff of wind blows papers and ads for Kroger’s and Western Auto across the yard. I bend to pick them up like I’m fielding ground balls, though I haven’t played a game of ball for years. “A frivolous waste of time,” says Bertha about the game I used to love.

I stuff blown papers into the barrel. Josephine’s child-like handwriting is on an envelope, addressed to me. It’s been opened. I read, “Since I don’t hear from you, I guess Daddy don’t give you my letters. Still root for the Cards? Your prob-ably too big to act out games like you used to. Are you handsome as Rock Hudson? I died my hair black. You wouldn't know me. Come see me if you can."

The match book cover gives a restaurant's name and address: Fifth Street Diner, St. Charles, Missouri. Bertha, you and I are gonna have a long talk. *Why did you keep Josephine's letters from me?* But first, I'll go visit Jo.

That evening I tell Dad my first lie in a long time, that I have an appointment to see a doctor about glasses. The following afternoon, I climb off a Greyhound bus in St. Charles. The match book cover map shows Jefferson as the cross street.

Noon rush is over. The afternoon shift about to come to work. I hope Jo's still there. Inside, booths are situated along the right side beneath long, low windows. The dining room is yellow Formica tables and chairs, with stainless steel legs. The counter is at the back, next to the kitchen.

Josephine and two ladies are in a back booth counting coins and cussing customers. The cigarette ash tray needs emptying. Josephine muddy brown eyes find me. "Whatcha want?"

"How about a kiss Josephine Marie Holt? I'm your brother, Jeremy."

"Jeremy?' She eyes me. "Rock Hudson don't have to worry. Where'd ya get them pimples? How'd you get here?"

"Took the Weekly," I say, hoping she'll remember that's how she got home a long time ago. She doesn't make the connection. She's chewed her lip stick off. Black mascara is in big lumps on her lashes. Her black hair frames an old face.

"Wait at the counter," she says, shoving three quarters at me. "Have a hamburger on me. They're good. I'll be off in fifteen."

* * *

We go next door to a bar. She drinks Stag. Me 7-Up. We talk about the Cardinals and the weather and hair color and movie stars. The juke box plays Perry Como's *Round and Round,* followed by Pat Boone and *Love Letters in the Sand.* It's been almost five years since I last saw her.

"Daddy and Bertha got married," I say. "The dairy's doing good, but it's hard work. We milk 42 Holsteins twice a day. Added on to the house. Bertha sleeps in one new room. Curt and his wife in the other. She's from Germany. She strips the cows after the milking machine has finished with them. She throws ten-gallon milk cans around like a man." I'm talking to break the silence. "Dad's still in your room."

Jo nods. She puffs on her Pall Mall. "You're still not an uncle, yet. 'Cept for . . ." She doesn't finish the sentence. "Guess I can't have kids. My divorce came through. Second one." Her eyes search mine. "I'm damaged goods now, for sure." She laughs. "Write sometime, okay?"

I lie that I will.

Her face works. "Think Daddy would let me come home?"

This surprises me. "Why? We work 14 – 16 hours a day. Every day."

"Should've married Curt when I had a chance. He'd been a good husband." She makes a clicking sound with her mouth. "I cook now. Big city life is all go, go. No time to just sit."

"Sure," I say. "C'mon on home. Why not? You can have your old room back. Dad'll sleep in the tack room with me." More lies. *What the hell. She's my sister.*

'One last time," I say, "do I just vant to be left alone. Like that actress you used to mimic."

"Jeez, Jeremy. Grow up, ya little shrimp." She almost

smiles.

I touch her hand. "Tell ya what. Meet me at Greyhound tomorrow morning. 9:05. We'll go home together. I'll have you a ticket."

Jo makes her eyes go big. "Bernie's usually gone by then. I'll be there."

I don't ask who Bernie is. I should have, I guess.

Josephine smiles. For a minute she looks like the girl I remember, young and pretty, not old, divorced, with black hair.

* * *

I wait at the Greyhound station for Jo. Our bus leaves. She doesn't show. I go to the Fifth Street Diner.

"She wasn't here for her shift," the manager says, lighting a Camel. "If new girls don't get the breakfast shift or pull in the tips they think they should, they move on in a hurry."

"She was here at least a month."

"Same difference."

He doesn't know who Bernie is. The only address he has for her is General Delivery, St. Charles. No telephone number. "Sorry, bud. That's life."

What can I do? If I go to the police they'll want an address, who she lives with, why I think she might be in danger. To them, she just didn't show up to work on time. I go back to Greyhound and wait for the next bus.

Maybe she and Bernie made up. Maybe she changed her mind when she heard how hard we work at the dairy. Maybe she'll come home when the mood hits her.

I climb off the Greyhound four hours later in Yellowbird. At home, Dad asks, "Where ya been?" He smells like a gut wagon from the booze.

"Bus ran late."

"That don't tell me dick. Where was ya?"

"Eye doctor's. Had an appointment. Remember?"

He weaves back and forth, his eyes vacant. "Hell, yes. I 'member. Jist checkin'." John Barleycorn has him. He'll pass out across his bed again tonight.

Now that I'm home, I realize there's no reason to talk to Bertha about why she kept Josephine's letters from me. She'd deny she got more than one letter, or say she meant to tell me, but forgot, and it won't happen again. There's nothing I can do about how she treats me. A year from now when I'm eighteen, I'll join the Army and disappear like Josephine.

* * *

It's Milred's day off. She gets two a month. In the kitchen I dice an onion and toss it in a skillet with butter. When it's brown, I add three slices of Spam, put mustard on two slices of Holsum bread. When the Spam curls a little, I ladle it up, add pickle relish. Josephine's favorite dish.

I eat at the kitchen table, looking out at the maple tree where years before Jo told me about her baby boy, and how someone stole him from her the day he was born. *What would Momma have said to her? What did I say?*

How old would her boy be now. Five? Six? Yeah, six. He'll never run these hills, fish these creeks or milk these cow. I laugh. *Maybe that's a good thing.*

After I've eaten, I sit for a while thinking of Mom and Jo. I miss them both. *A nephew would be great to have around. I'd show him how to hit a baseball.* I rinse my dishes.

What did Mr. Toad in Willows say when he got tired?

Onion sauce. I smile. Soon, I'll say the same. But for now, mornings come early on a dairy. I head for my rack in the tack room.

The End

WINNER TAKE ALL

WINNER TAKE ALL

It's fight night and my friend Ryman Call is gettin' clobbered to a bloody mess by young Bob Cleary. Blood drips from Ryman's chin, his right eye swole big as a persimmon. Bob Cleary circles him, a hungry wolf after a crippled sheep. Cleary sends a hard left to Ryman's forehead. Ryman staggers like a toddler tryin' to walk, a right smashes into his belly. Ryman sprawls to the sawdust.

Cleary waves his fists over his head like he's the new champ. The crowd screams and stomps, glad Ryman Call is finally gettin' his due, plum tickled the local boy they've watched trot off to school holdin' big sister's hand, is doin' the smashin', they yell, "Get up, Ryman. Get up!" They want him beat on more.

I'm Hamas Zanderhook. I cook for Ryman and his three daughters and ride herd on Winder, his eight-year-old boy. I seen ere one of his slugfests from his first barroom brawl to tonight's donnybrook. This is the onlyist time he's ever ate sawdust. Usually, it's the other feller who's covered with blood and snot and will mebbe cripple through life the rest of his days.

Ryman's shellackin' pains me terrible. If I had my druthers I'd grab Lon Warfield's pistol and shoot Bob Cleary 'tween the eyes, but Ryman would yell, "Stay outta my rock patch, Zee."

Sweaty palms and stingin' eyes be hanged, I gotta a job to do, so I climb into the Big Money seats to handle the bettin' needs of the gentlemen there. A soft-handed feller in a gray fedora, pushes two Abe's at me. I give him a marker and grab five Washington's from a city boy with thick glasses and new shoes.

A farmer in the standin' section yells, "Dummy, get yer ass over here."

I duck under the rope and take his greenbacks. Ryman lays in the dust like a lazy dog. The farmer's moola is probably all he has left from that load of hay he sold last fall, stashin' the rolled-up bills in a Prince Albert tobacco can in the barn rafters, should Baby Sister's headaches return, and the doc needs to visit, or the vet comes durin' calvin' season.

"Mark me for three bucks, Dummy. All Ryman's gonna win tonight is a trip to the cemetery."

I write, "3 bucks. Redheaded farmer. New overalls." on my paper, scrawl $3 on 'nother sheet and hand it to him. He'll get his money back, 'long with matching funds from Ryman's wad if Bob Cleary holds his gains, which I hope he don't.

For the fighter's it's winner take all. Knock the other guy senseless or make him cry uncle and ya take home the pot. Ever penny, which could sit ya up fer life. My cigar box is jammed with seven, eight hunnert bucks, not countin'

Ryman's seed money.

Truth be told, folks are more 'n a little surprised at how this fandango's unfurled, even if they hoped it'd be this way. But, hope's one thing, and real somethin' different.

On the fight floor, Bob Cleary yells, "Get up, Old Man. I got more where that come from." Ryman pulls hisself to one knee, but looks like he ain't got the strength, nor the juice to spit.

* * *

Ridin' over from Yellowbird in Lon Warfield's pickup earlier this evenin', Ryman said, "These boys got money to burn. We've an obligation to see it goes in our pocket, so they won't start no unsafe fires."

That's Ryman. All jokes and razzin' 'cept when he's beatin' the sap outta some young man with more moolah than brains. He's lucky to just get knocked out. Some of Ryman's victims limp through life after a go at him. Some lose a eye, get a broke back or collapsed lung 'cause they keep gettin' up after Ryman hammers 'em to the ground. One young man spends his days strapped to a chair, prayin' the next spasm won't be as hard as the last one. There's no room for pride when death stalks the ring.

Now, Bob Cleary struts, the prettiest rooster in the coop, hopin' Ryman stands, so he can knock him from here to St. Louis and be rich as a bank robber from the prize money.

* * *

This fist throwin' contest come 'bout nigh onto two months ago. I brung a mess of fresh carrots onto the back porch. Ryman waved a envelop at me. “Cleary’s answer,” he says. “I’ll whup his ass the first Saturday in June. At his bailiwick.”

He thumbs a stamp on the letter. “Goin’ by the post office the next day or two, Zee? Drop this off would ya?”

Since Ryman’s doin’ the askin’, I whoop up my mule, Pete Grey, and we clippety-clop into Yellowbird, where Miss Hattie McCormack, the post mistress, drops the letter into the mail bag. Miss Hattie’s a special friend. She taught me finger talk. My ears may be scarred and orange as a dried apricot, but I hear just fine. It were my talk box that got burned away in the house fire that kilt baby sister Darcy and turned Pap to a black cinder. The onlyist sounds I can manage are mouth noises, hisses, grunts and lip pops.

Some years ago, Miss Hattie held up a book when she seen me. “This shows how to spell words using fingers. If we both learn, you can tell me your needs, not waste time with motions and hissing sounds.”

That were ‘bout when the schoolmarm said my scarred-ugly face made little one’s pee they’s pants, and either I stop comin’ to school, or she’d quit. It were no contest, so Miss Hattie learned me to read and do my sums, me spellin’ the answers with my fingers. That were a blessin’ most as big as Ryman’s generosity, I tell you.

Miss Hattie asks, “Hamas, your still going to move to Jeff City to look for your Momma?”

I spell out, “Most likely. When Winder’s in school.”

She nods. “Good time as any to dig up old bones, I guess. Remember, Young Man, just because your Momma was seen in the Katy railroad depot wearing high heels and a party dress doesn’t mean she’s a Katy Lady.”

I nod. Soft words don’t change hard facts. Mom liked

her drink when she lived with me and Pap and Darcy, so bein' a Katy Lady fits her like a Saturday night dance. Katy Ladies comfort lonely men travelers on the railroad. The ladies ride free and share their earnin's with the conductor.

I spell out, "That's where I'll start."

Miss Hattie nods. "I'm here if you need me."

"Thanks," I spell and climb on Pete, kickin' him to a trot. I'm in a hurry to get home and pick some tunes on my banjo to keep away bad thoughts.

* * *

When I first taken bed and founder with Ryman's family, he and Miss Ethel farmed 90 acres of Missouri River bottom land, south and east of Yellowbird. Dirt farmin's never easy, but the summer of '32, it got worse. Them bankers at the Yellowbird National Bank stole Ryman's inheritance, nigh to $9,000, and closed the bank doors for good. Come spring, Ol' Muddy flooded for the fourth straight year and washed away Ryman's crops. Money gets scarce when yer seeds, yer out buildin's, even yer cows, float downstream to New Orleans, leavin' piles of sand and bloated fish where tall corn oughta grow.

Toppin' off these miseries, Ryman's sweet wife, Miss Ethel, she who nursed me back to health when I were burned, passed away the fall of '41, leavin' Ryman with three daughters and Winder to raise without a woman's touch. He come to Jeff City where I were playin' the banjo for The Music Freaks, the group we crippled musicians put together. "I need ya at home, Boy." I been his cook and chore doer since.

Now, the fifth day of June 1943, Bob Cleary parades hands over his head, like the King of Prussia, pretendin' he's the new bare-knuckle champ of Callaway County. Come Saturday night he hopes to waltz into Yellowbird, the ladies smilin' all big at him, eager to hop in the buggy and go for a ride. He just needs to salt Ryman Call away. That's all.

* * *

A little over two hours ago, Lon Warfield parked his pickup under the big maples next to the IGA Warehouse. Ryman climbed out, stretched and touched his toes. Ten or twelve fight fans, come early to get good seats, boo like Ryman's a Halloween ghost, hot as a railroad spike left in the sun for the local fighter.

"Yer jest a fart in a windstorm 'round here, Ryman," one yells. 'Nother hollers, "Yer dead an' don't know it. Lay down. Make it easy on the undertaker."

Ryman waves. "Sorry to ruin yer party, boys, but I'm gonna send yer feller home with his tail 'tween his legs." He laughs, but he's serious as sin.

Word that champion Ryman Call has arrived travels fast. 'Fore ya can say May, June and July, a dozen or so more beer-drinkin' fight fans hot-foot over from the Harvest Moon Bar. They figure Ryman'll get his ass kicked, but who don't want to gander at the king 'fore he's knocked from his throne?

Addin' sugar to the spice, the feller they figger to do the knockin' is a youngster they seen climb onto his momma's lap on Market Day, unbutton her dress, say "Tit" and take his dinner. Don't that make Ryman's demise even more grand?

* * *

Me, Lon Warfield and 9-year-old Winder, my special

charge at his Daddy's fights, are invisible to these folks. They eye Ryman like a prize bull when he crosses the parkin' lot and goes inside for the usual pre-fight confab.

Lon Warfield, Ryman's driver, melts into the crowd, pistol in his pocket. Ryman says, "Lon's quiet as a Indian and smart as a owl. He can gut and skin a deer 'fore the air leaves it's lungs."

Inside, Ryman ponies up a hunnert dollars to Tom Baker, the fight timekeeper. The local boy hands Tom five hunnert smackeroos for the honor of gettin' the hominy-grit shit beat outta him. Tom drops the Jing-a-ling into a bag and straps it to his leg where it'll stay 'til a clear winner's declared.

Rich folks from Columbia and Jeff City, mebbe even St. Louis, park Fords, Chevys, and Desoto's, along the gravel road in front of the IGA Warehouse. Inside, they wash down hamburgers and hotdogs and guzzle Griesedieck Brothers beer. They don't give a hang who wins this rumpus long as they got money on the winner. They wear blue or tan pants and white short-sleeve shirts open at the neck and smoke store-bought cigarettes.

The local boys hobble their wagon team in the pasture behind the warehouse, wearin' fresh-ironed overalls and blue shirts, heavy shoes or boots wiped clean of cow manure and horse dust. They're bettin' the neighbor boy beats the royal shit out of Ryman Call tonight and if they take a fiver, mebbe even a ten-spot home to the little lady, that ain't no sin, right?

After Ryman agreed to this shindig, he learned Bob Cleary were fifteen years younger, five inches taller and mebbe fifty pounds heavier'n him. "He hits like a fallin' tree, with arms long as a mowin' blade. His last three fights, he knocked out good men in less than seven minutes. Total. He's got sparkle."

Ryman laughs. "Yah fer him. A good fight means a happy crowd and folks eager to turn out fer our next knuckle-throwin' party. And more greenback dollars to feed my family."

Ryman'll fight a giant and two midgets at the same time, if the money's right. Tonight, he's got to handle a big, strong feller in his own backyard, with the crowd yellin' encouragement ever fist he throws. That's a heavy load even for champion Ryman Call.

For Cleary, this fight's like candy from Santa Claus. Hell, Ryman's old enough to be his daddy. He's gonna get whupped sometime, so why not tonight? Winnin' the pot is the difference 'tween drivin' a Farmall tractor come plowin' time, or lookin' a sway-backed mule in the ass 'nother year. Plus, Cleary aims to ladle gravy on his taters from side bets won from them who don't think he's got the goods to handle Ryman Call.

As the never-been-whupped-top-dog in the county, Ryman names where the fight's to be held and when. He don't fight in Yellowbird 'cause he knows even if you been to our fair town afore, crows get lost lookin' for our slice of Heaven. We got more hills than hollers, and if the road ain't washed out and muddy, its rocky, with so many twists and turns you think you're goin' forward, when you're really goin' backards.

As for how many rounds to fight, for tonight's get go, Ryman named 5 twenty minute rounds with a twenty minute blow in between. If both fighters still stand after all that fist-throwin', they take ten minutes to piss and gulp down a beer or two, then battle 'til one of 'em quits or goes down and stays down.

The rules agreed to, I tag along when Ryman walks the

fight place, Winder holdin' my thumb like a chicken leg. *I'll miss that boy when I'm gone, I tell you.*

Sawdust is spread on the fresh-oiled wood floor. It smells like smoke and kerosene. Two yellow light bulbs dangle from black cords in the center of the room where the gladiators come to mark. A cellar door, two hickory saplin's nailed 'cross it, leans agin the far wall, transportation to the sawbones, if needed, and most fighters do after Ryman's busted 'em up.

Healthy young ladies with big bosoms sell dime hot dogs and hamburgers, washed down with 15-cent beer from booths roped off agin the wall. Wood benches form a square where the fighters mix it up toward the center of the room. If ya ain't got a buck for a bench seat up front, four bits buys ya a place to stand, along the wall on both sides clean back to the shelves. Jake Atteberry, the IGA store owner, oughta slip Ryman a Franklin or two since the hope that Ryman'll get his ass whupped is why folks have piled in here tonight, thick as sinners at a church revival.

After the walk-through, me and Winder follow Ryman to Lon's pick up, where he changes into tight black pants with a red cloth belt and high-top canvas shoes. He trots up the road a hunnert yards or so and back, a bevy of school boys runnin' long side, chatterin' like blue jays.

"I'm gonna be a fighter when I grow up." And, "Knock the shit outta him, Mr. Call." Back at the truck, Ryman does jumpin' jacks, dabs Vaseline on his eyebrows, 'round his ears and nose, slicks his red hair back with pomade and trots to the fight place. I pocket the Vaseline for later use, help Winder shoulder his Daddy's stool, and carry Ryman's ice bucket and towels, Winder by my side.

When Ryman enters the fight place, fight fans yell cat

calls. "Ya'll look like that freak next to ya 'fore the night's over." That's meant for me, but don't bother me none. I know I'm ugly. 'Nother yell is, "Don't worry, Ryman. We'll take good care of ya. We got a hearse waitin' outside."

When the local hero marches in, the crowd cheers. He has I-hate-the-world-look on his whiskered face. He's monster big, mebbe 6 foot 4 or 5, a solid 250-260. His hair is bushy and black as a wolverine's, his squinty eyes, ice blue.

Ryman shuffles his feet in sawdust, then hustles out to the mark. Cleary comes up. He wears long underwear cut off at the waist and cinched with a wide leather belt, the drop seat to his union-alls sewed shut. He's bare-chested. Standin' next to him, Ryman looks like a lost school boy. Ryman says to Cleary, "Get yer last will and testament wrote, Shorty?"

The gong sounds. The big bruiser pops Ryman with a hard right. Ryman fires a straight left to let folks know he come to the dance. Cleary is a southpaw, a fighter who leads with his right hand. Ryman ain't seen this style 'fore, so his guard ain't good as it should be. Cleary's jabs sound horse-whip loud agin Ryman's face and arms. When Ryman lands a punch, Cleary grunts.

Ryman says, "Lookin' for yer Momma? She's down at the creek showin' her hairy thang a dime a look." He hopes this will rile the young fighter, so he'll throw wild punches and wear hisself out. Cleary just grins.

Round one ends. Neither fighter has a clear advantage, but things change faster than a left jab in round two. The big boy is on Ryman like dust on a tobacco plant.

I 'spec Ryman's put out by this, 'cause most fights he knocks some poor sucker out while the gong still quivers, then chugs beer in the tavern, his winnin's piled on the bar, eyein' the local talent, decidin' which lucky girl will be his tonight.

Tonight's merry-go-round is a hump and a holler from Ryman's first lollapalooza. That were one Saturday night at the Pick and Shovel Bar in Mokane. Ryman was enjoyin' a cold beer after a hard week's work, when them Hatton brothers marched in. They pointed at a certain farmer's wife, sayin' they'd sure like a go with her and her sittin' right there next to her husband eatin' a cheeseburger.

When her man rose to defend her honor, Tim Hatton busted the farmer's nose wide open with one punch, hammered him to the floor and kicked in his ribs. This riled Ryman, who seen the whole thing.

He told Tim Hatton he were wrong to blackguard in front of a lady and to apologize to her. Tim said, "Make me. Old Man."

His brother, Tom, laughed. "Mind yer own bidness, Old Man, or we'll beat the Shinola outta of ya."

Ryman said, "So that's the way it is, huh?" He turned like he were gonna walk away, then wheeled and landed two punches. Both brothers skidded agin a booth clear 'cross the room, out cold as a lantern with no oil.

Tom Baker, an up-and comin' feller, got wind of this little tussle. Tuesday evenin' he come a-callin'. He told Ryman they was a challenge fight in Jeff City that comin' Saturday night and Ryman could win twenty bucks if he won the whole thing. "That'd buy my girls new winter clothes," he said.

Saturday night, Ryman's punch 'bout ripped the other fighter's head off his shoulders. He pocketed most onto thirty bucks from the pot and side bets. He given Tom Baker a fiver for the tip. Tom hisself, made some serious moola bettin' on Ryman. In addition, for actin' as timekeeper and fight master, the White Moon bar owner given him a ten.

The followin' week, at Tom's urgin', Ryman signed on

for a six-man slam bang. This is where each fighter puts up a ten spot. The last one standin' wins it all. "Fifty dollars buys seed come plantin' time," Ryman said.

Tom Baker pocketed a ten spot from the bar owners for bossin' the whole affair, plus a buck from each fighter for bein' the timekeeper and he done right good bettin' Ryman would clean everone's plow, which he did. Since that night to this, Tom time-keeps for Ryman's fights and he knows who to bet akin.

Eddie Kepler and his wife Claudette got wind of this Free for All. Eddie were all the time braggin' he could knock over a outhouse with one blow of his big fist. He figured the prize money would buy new suckers for they's well pump, and Claudette cottoned a new red dress from J.C. Penney. And lipstick.

They took 10 rainy-day smackeroos from the Clabber Girl Baking Soda can on the top shelf in the kitchen cabinet and dropped it into the jar on the bar at the Wise Owl in Ashland. Eddie musta have thought he'd be found the fast road to riches when he knocked out the local butcher in his first go 'round.

In his second match Eddie laid out the preacher's son with two punches. When Eddie seen his next opponent were Ryman Call, his eyes lit up, convinced this would be a duck soup go for him. After all, Ryman were probably forty-years old, and Eddie just turned twenty-five.

'Fore the fight, Eddie sidled up to Ryman. "I got a ten spot that says I whup yer ass, Old Man. Can ya match it?"

The way bets 'tween fighters are supposed to be handled is the timekeeper holds the money and pays off the winner. When Eddie didn't follow this rule, Ryman grinned, figurin' Eddie didn't have the gettis to back his bet.

"Yer on, Youngster," Ryman said.

Tom Baker hit the gong. Eddie came out swingin'. Ryman swatted his blows away like they was smoke rings, then slapped Eddie like a daddy does to correct his son. This angrified Eddie. He commenced to throw rights and lefts, missin' Ryman here to Minnesota. After mebbe five minutes, his face welted and red from Ryman's slaps, pantin' like a dog chasin' rabbits, sweat drippin' from his chin, Eddie drops his guard.

Ryman slaps him twice more. Hard. Eddie stands still as a fence post. Ryman tousles his hair like he were a youngster, then unloads a right to his chin. Bones snap. Blood flies. Eddie falls.

Ten minutes and two buckets of cold water later, he sits up, spits out a tooth and asks, "Where am I?"

"In my shit house," Ryman says. "Where's my ten bucks?"

His lips bloody, his tongue playin' in the hole where his tooth were, Eddie whines, "Mr. Call, could ya kindly give me a few days? I'll sell a load of wood or somethin' to pay ya."

Ryman says, "Sure, I could do that. But, I won't. If I did, I'd have forty-seven challengers in three minutes from every asshole with two fists and no money in his pocket. You made the bet, boy. Pay up."

"Wouldja take my mules?"

"Naw, I got a good team. 'Sides, how'd ya plow come spring?"

Eddie don't answer.

Ryman says, "Got a cow?"

Eddie shakes no.

"Too, bad," Ryman says.

Ryman eyes Claudette, Eddie's wife, who's wipin' blood from her husband's face, her face white as a rag. "Ya countenance his bet," Ryman asks.

Claudette flutters blue eyes at Ryman. "No sir. He often does stupid things on his own." She pushes a blonde curl behind her ear.

Ryman says. "Eddie, yer wife worth ten bucks?"

Eddie lets out a long breath. Claudette waits for Eddie to answer, a smile on her red lips. When Eddie don't open his yap, she says, "Ya damn right, I am. Got a car? Or will our wagon bed do?"

* * *

Good fighters don't beg. For years, Ryman Call's beat the goose feathers off ever fighter he's faced, but tonight he's gettin' pay back. He's got two choices. One, stay in the saw-dust and not come to mark the next round, so that Bob Cleary wins the pot, or he gets up and Bob Cleary creams him. Again. That's how his cards stack up.

Bob Cleary, on his part, celebrates like it's his birth-day, certain he won the fight. He blows kisses to the crowd and does backflips, jumps in the air, shakes his fist at Ryman and does a jig.

While he's doin' all this, Ryman scrambles on all fours to the far corner of the fight floor, and stands, his guard up. There's more'n one way to de-nut a hog, he figgers.

Cleary spies Ryman and comes runnin'. "Yer mine, Old Man, yer mine."

Ryman greets Bob with a straight left to the jaw and a right to the heart, but his punches ain't got snap. He uses rasslin' holds to keep Cleary off balance 'til the gong sounds.

Cleary skips back to his stool, happy as a schoolgirl. He

punches the air mebbe fifty times, certain he'll knock Ryman into next week when the next round starts. His brothers pound his back and call him "Champ," eager for the fight purse and side bet money to fill they's pockets. All that's left is for Bob to coldcock Ryman. That's all.

* * *

Ryman slumps on his stool, dusty as a railroad hobo, blood oozin' from a cut over his right eye. He watches Cleary celebrate. "Go ahead, boy," he whispers. "Wear yerself out."

Ryman pulls me close. "Any idees?"

I shake no. I ain't a corner man like boxin' glove fighters have, a fight-smart feller who stops blood from a cut and gives his fighter advice. I can't talk, much less make swellins' go down. Who am I with a scarred face and brittle skin to tell Ryman Call how to fight? 'Sides, he needs to get his piss and vinegar back to win this little quarrel.

Ryman has 'nother problem as well. If he lasts 'nother round, he'll have to fight 'til him or Cleary, one or the other, goes down and stays down. That ain't good. Ryman's right eye is swole up like wasps held a stingin' contest on him, his chest and arms covered with red welts and purple bruises. Sawdust sticks to his shoulders. He's wet from sweat. He'll piss claret for a week when this is over.

Will tonight be the first time ever Ryman Call don't come to scratch, his time as champion over?

Winder stands soldier-straight behind his Daddy's stool, his fists clenched, his knuckles white, fightin' tears. Lon Warfield pushes through the crowd to gander at Ryman. His face goes pale. He don't speak, just turns and heads outside to see the moon, rather than watch Ryman get knocked silly.

Ryman Call's the best man I've ever knowed. He found me cold, wet and bad burned, yet he brung me home. His wife, Miss Ethel, patched me up. Since that day to this, seven years have passed. I've slept under Ryman's roof and filled my belly at his table. Now, he's a goner, and they's no help I can give him.

* * *

Ryman pulls me close. "Think I outta use my crippled quail?"

What Ryman means is he'll act like one of Cleary's punches hurts him bad, the way a momma quail pretends she has a broke wing when you get too close to her babies. She'll flutter 'long the ground just outta reach. When you've followed her fifteen or twenty feet, and her brood's safe, her wing gets a magic cure and off she flies, fast as a Indian arrow. That's what Ryman means.

I nod and poke the air with my right and fire a left. Ryman says, "Gotcha. I ain't thrown a decent one all night."

The crowd commences to laugh. I turn. Two boys, one dressed like a scarecrow, the other like a old woman, stand near me.

"Yer a ugly son-a-bitch," Scarecrow says.

I can't argue. *It's true. Folks suspicion the fire that scarred me bad was started by my own momma since she ain't been seen in these parts since that night, That is 'til last month when she were spied at the Katy station in Jeff City.*

I offer my hand to Scarecrow, like his joke's fun. He tosses a cup of liquid at me. By the smell, it's coal oil. The Old Woman's match flames out 'fore a fire ignites. Folks slap they's knees and laugh. It ain't funny to me.

Now, I know I gotta find my momma and learn if she

started the fire that killed Darcy and Pap.

A fight fan from the big money seats hustles up, grabs the boys and pulls 'em outside. "Idiots," he says. "You'll burn the whole place down."

Ryman says, "Pay 'em no mind, Zee."

Easy for him to say, but it's me they made laughin' stock of.

Winder says, "Ya ain't ugly, Hamas. And yer sure nice to me."

That may be true, but I gotta face my past.

* * *

The gong sounds. Round five. Bob Cleary rushes out, eyes gleamin,' ready to put Ryman asleep. He fires punches like they cancelled tomorrow and he's the onlyist one to know it.

Ryman grabs and holds on, so Bob's fists hit only his arms and shoulders, his blows don't seem to have steam like earlier. *He celebrate too much?*

Ryman lands a right hook to Cleary's belly. Cleary backs off, probably surprised at Ryman's get up and go. Me, too. Then, Ryman slaps Cleary. The crowd roars.They know this is Ryman sayin' settle yer bets boys, I got the reins. This fight's mine.

Cleary's eyes go big. He flings a right. Ryman blocks it and slaps him agin. Cleary charges Ryman like a Arkansas razorback goin' for a slop trough. Ryman dances away. Cleary's left glances his shoulder. Ryman slaps Cleary agin.

"Ya dumb sonavabitch," Cleary yells. He fires 'nother right, 'nother left, 'nother right but hits only air.

"Stand still," he yells at Ryman.

Cleary zings a left, a right, a left. Ryman blocks 'em all. Cleary's eyes glint like a badger chasin' a chicken. He fires a long right to Ryman's forehead. Ryman goes down like he were shot. Cleary yells, "Get up, Ol' man. I'm gonna wreck ya!"

Cleary waves to the crowd, and hops 'round like a grasshopper on a fryin' pan. Ryman drags hisself to the far corner of the fight floor, and stands, wavin' like a persimmon sprout in the wind. Cleary rushes him. Ryman feints with his right. Bob Cleary's eyes follow this fist for a hiccup, 'after all that's the one that's served poison all night.

Ryman's left hook sizzles in over Cleary's right shoulder and smashes agin his jaw. Cleary's mouth pops open. Teeth drop to the dirt. Blood spurts.

It's hard to knock out a man as big as Bob Cleary with one punch. Ryman knows time's runnin' out, but he can't hurry. He sends a hard right to Cleary's nose. The sound of snapped bone causes fans to flinch. Blood gushes from Cleary's face like tomatoes from a jar. Ryman's left sends Cleary to the sawdust.

Cleary gazes up at Ryman, his mouth open. He shakes his head to chase away this bad dream. A short breath earlier, it was Ryman Call who was down. Now, probably wagon wheels float 'fore Cleary's eyes, salty blood fills his mouth.

Cleary staggers to his feet. Ryman bangs a right hook to his kidney. *Can Ryman finish Cleary 'fore the gong sounds?*

Cleary lunges at Ryman. He knows his neighbor's bet good money that he'd win this scuffle, money meant to buy a new calf, or shingle the smokehouse. He wants one clear punch at Ryman, so they can collect their bets and go home rich. He probably hates the place where minutes earlier, he were king.

"Stand still, Coward," he yells at Ryman.

Over by by his stool, Cleary's brothers are helpless as 'possums in a tree. One kneels, chewin' the towel he waved a short minute ago. The older brother closes his eyes, but that don't stop the sound of that son-of-a-bitch Ryman Call firing punch-after-punch into Brother's broken body.

The crowd's quiet as a church at collection time. They came to see the new king crowned, not watch him get beat bloody. *Why'd I bet agin Ryman, they probably ask.* Now, like water poured on fresh-plowed ground, that money's gone, takin' the new garden plow and hog wire fence with it.

Bob Cleary's arms dangle at his side. Blood covers his chest and belly. He turns from the waist to follow Ryman. Tom Baker raises his hammer, ready to signal the fight's end. Ryman pops Cleary with a hard right. Yet Cleary stands, a gnarled tree with strong roots.

Ryman rears back to deliver a mighty blow. Instead, he shoves Cleary, who staggers, twists and falls. Ryman catches him and lowers him to the sawdust like he's layin' one of his precious daughters into bed for a long night's sleep.

The gong sounds. Cleary's brothers run out to carry him to his stool. "Ya win, ya son-of-a-bitch," the older brother says. "Bob's had 'nuff."

* * *

The crowd mutters like pigeons in a coop, bumpin' shoulders as they push out of the fight place, air smellin' like a over-turned privy. It ended so fast, some wonder what happened. One minute, the great Ryman Call was down. The next, they's hero's a sawdust-covered lump on the floor.

"Did Ryman fire a left and a right, or two lefts," a man asks. Some of the big city boy's faces are pale, like they have a touch of ague comin' on.

At Lon's truck, Ryman pays Tom Baker ten dollars for his time-keepin', plus a fiver for gas. He probably made 'nother fifty or sixty on side bets. Tom's wife is Baptist, so he'll head home. Ryman'll settle with Lon Warfield later.

Ryman says, "That left ya suggested were a good idee, Zee. Had to damn near kill him 'fore he went down." He shakes his head. "Ain't this a nasty game? Beat someone 'til they can't walk, all for money."

He's never said anything like that 'fore now. Ryman towels blood off and changes into clean overalls and shirt. I rub Vaseline on cuts over his eyes and stow his fight gear in Lon's truck, grab my banjo and follow him and Winder into the Harvest Moon. We ain't got no bets to settle, since we won 'em all.

Inside the music box plays Bob Wills and his Texas Playboys, *Please Don't Leave Me.* Folks stand on the dance floor. A path clears when Ryman comes up. A girl in a flowered skirt and red high heels stands on tip toes to kiss Ryman's black eye. "I'd take good care of ya," she says.

"You're a pretty thing," Ryman says, givin' her a squeeze. Mebbe ten young men come up. A boy in a white shirt and straw hat says, "Won me forty-three dollars tonight, Mr. Call. Much obliged."

"Good for you," Ryman says. "'Bout what I'm takin' home. But ya got yer's without spillin' a drop of blood." Everone laughs.

We climb onto bar stools. Roy Acuff's *Beautiful Brown Eyes* plays on the jukebox. The sweet scent of Midnight in Paris perfume mixes with cigarette smoke and beer. A pretty redhead stands kissin' close to Ryman.

"Hear you're quite the dancer," she says.

Ryman touches his swollen eye. “Not tonight, honey. ‘Nother time I’ll show you a few moves.” She rolls her big brown eyes and shakes her head.

I drink red soda pop while Winder guzzles Dr. Pepper. Ryman drains his Griesedieck and stands. “Let’s go, boys. Been a long night.”

Me and Winder climb into Lon’s pick up. I pull the tarp up to our neck. Winder rests his head on my shoulder. He’s asleep ‘fore we cross the railroad tracks. Stars fill the sky. The air is warm and heavy, but I shiver and shake all the way home.

The End

THE SUMMER SLAVE

THE SUMMER SLAVE

The rancid smell of chicken droppings, a Missouri sun turning a tin roof chicken coop hot as charcoal, sweat stinging my eyes, I step into knee-high smoldering weeds hoping to catch a cool breeze. My coat is covered with chicken feathers, dried dung and flecks of whitewash. My head throbs. I could drink a river dry. *Where's that well I saw earlier?*

I have only myself to blame for my predicament. I was so eager to impress my new host family that I made a rookie mistake and started work before getting the ground rules straight. I know better. Today, June 19, 1951, marks my fourth year as a summer slave. I hope it's my last.

Brother Seymour, from the Home, preaches to always know the rules before picking up a shovel. If I'd followed his advice, I wouldn't have to search for water, I'd know how my laundry is handled, have an agreed-on work schedule, and where the nearest swimming hole is.

I need water. Fast.

Mrs. Keller rapped on my door at 6 o'clock sharp this morning. "Up, Arthur, up." Her face clouded over like a dirty mirror when I stood under the maples, dressed, ready for the day. In the kitchen, I suck down Post Toasties in warm milk, while she recites my chores like a teacher taking class room roll.

My first assignment? Clean the chicken coops. I don't ask questions, just grab a broom, shovel, paint brush, white-wash and hop to it. I finished them and I'm ready for a break. I see the well under tall maples through broadleaf weeds and wet grass.

I wonder. Is the water safe to drink? At the well I turn the handle. Brown liquid spells out. If I could sing, I would. This shows the well's in use. I spin the handle again. Cool water splashes out. I rinse my face and hands, then drink straight from the spigot. *Now maybe I'll last till noon.*

I pull my shirt from my coat pocket and dry my face. When I open my eyes, a brown-skinned girl with gobs of black hair stands beside me. "You the new orphan?"

Her voice hints of Carmina Maranda. I give her the once over. At the Home, guys would pay a nickel to watch her climb the stairs to the girl's dorm. A dime, if she was in Phys ed clothes.

White sandals. Brown feet. Slender toes. Red nail polish. Long, tan legs. Blue shorts. Yellow blouse tied below round breasts. Golden throat. Dark eyes. Thick black hair. More Cyd Charisse than Ava Gardner. *Is this the little snip Mrs. Keller warned me about last night?*

I answer. "Guilty. Want my autograph?"

She laughs. "Hi, I'm Fatima." She's the snip all right.

"Hi, Fatima. I'm Art."

She hangs her bucket on the spigot. "Fill 'er up, sir."

Her bucket filled, she stretches tan legs out on the well head. The sun turns her hair gold and blue. She smells like flour. I rinse whitewash from my paint brush. My stomach rumbles. I'm breathing fast.

Fatima says, "What's wrong, Orphan Boy? You're green around the gills."

My mouth fills with saliva. *Don't puke, Carr. Not now.* Fatima tugs at my coat. "This is heavy as a truck tire. Get it off."

I wear it to protect my jeans from chicken grime, since I don't know how long before my laundry's done. I have no shirt under it. At the Home, a bare chest in mixed company gets extra KP. I push Fatima away.

"Don't be silly. I've seen scrawny chests before." She yanks at the coat.

My face is on fire. Cold chills race up my spine. Trees twirl. I could maybe recite the first three letters of the alphabet, but say my own name? Never. Cold water knocks me to hot grass.

A voice from a dark tunnel orders, "Get in the shade, Orphan Boy."

I sprawl under a Spiriva bush. Fatima refills her bucket and sits. When the world stops spinning, she asks like nothing happened. "Think they'll adopt you?"

Ah, the Big Question. It usually doesn't raise its ugly head so soon. I play it straight. "Nope. Most couples want babies, not teenagers. I'm just a slave rented out for twenty-five dollars a month for three months. The money's supposed to go into my account for when I leave the Home, but somehow expenses always eat it up. My brother, Dwayne, got $47.67 for five summers of hard work. I'll be seventeen in June. Graduate high school in January." *Where did that word garbage come from?*

Fatima nods. "So that's how it works. I'll be sixteen in October. Going to the Fair tomorrow?"

"I'd be a Commie rat if I didn't, right"

She smiles. "I have a date with Tony Aguilera. He's twenty-one. Drives a Studebaker. Works with Papi."

"Cradle robber, huh? Anywhere to swim around here?"

She ignores my first question. "Wild Horse River at Twin Rocks. Before Devil's Fall."

She hands me a cup. "Sip. Maybe Tony'll win me a Kewpie Doll. Mom and I are going shopping later. Need a new skirt and blouse. Been to town yet?"

"Yeah. Quite the metropolis. What's the population? Minus three?"

"Sip. Not chug." She grabs the cup.

"Not funny. Almost four thousand. You'll go back to school this fall, huh? I'd be a sophomore, but Papi says school's a waste for girls. I applied at A & W. They'll hire when school starts."

I'm about to say a high school diploma is important for poor kids, when Mrs. Keller's tall body blocks the sun. "Up, up, Arthur. Mr. Sunshine waits for no one."

She claps her hands like Brother Seymour sending a play into a football game. "You have your water, Fatima. Leave. Arthur has work to do." She waves her apron at Fatima, like she's shooing flies.

"Get your shirt on, Arthur. You're in the company of a lady. Mr. Keller will have a word with you when he comes home."

Thick fingers fumble with small buttons. When I look up, Fatima has disappeared into the heat waves.

* * *

I arrived in Wheatland around sundown yesterday, after fourteen cramped hours on a Trailways bus. The Keller's met me at the station and dragged me to a prayer service followed by a pot luck supper. The preacher introduced Mr. Keller as a war hero. He asked prayers for Mrs. Keller, so she can, "Impart Christian principles to the lost orphan she graciously took into her home, even if last year's boy was a bitter disappointment. Christians overcome hardship with sacrifice."

I know there's no chance the Special Blessing of Adoption that Brother Seymour talks about will happen to me. "These fine country folks need workers. You orphans need homes. Anticipate a Special Blessing. Work hard for your host family. Pray for them. Emulate Christ in all you do. Your prayers will be answered."

I fill my plate with tuna casserole, Cole slaw, fried chicken and sliced tomatoes.

Better grub that what the Home serves. I take my paper plate to a bench beside the gate leading to the cemetery. The local kids, most younger than me, stare at the orphan freak, snickering at whispered, private jokes.

In the car, Jeff Tom says, "Daddy's head mechanic at a garage in town. I'll tell you what work you have to do."

This should have been my clue to get clear about what's expected of me, but since he's just a kid, I just nod. Now, my shirt buttoned to the collar, Mrs. Keller says, "Jeff Tom needs you in the hog pen."

Like that's a wonderful place, and I'm especially chosen by the Lord of the Manor. I figure his chores can't be as bad as white-washing chicken coops.

Wrong.

Jeff Tom asks, "Whatcha talkin' to that Mexican slut

for?"

"She saved my life."

Jeff Tom looks at me like I said little green men from Mars are coming for Sunday dinner, shrugs and says, "Momma lets her get water twice a day. Her folks rent our trailer. Thirty dollars a month. They never pay on time."

I saw the trailer on the weed-grown lot east of the house when we drove in last night. Maybe twenty feet long, five or six feet wide, rust holes along the side and four flat tires.

Jim Tom said, "Seven people live there. The parents. Two mean boys. A girl and her worthless husband. Momma says she'll squirt out a kid soon. And Fatima."

Mrs. Keller adds, "I'm warning you, Arthur. Fatima's a snip. Stay away from her."

I could say I've seen better places in a St. Louis slum but keep my mouth shut. Now, after a morning of hard labor, Jeff Tom hands me a broom. "Evander has a show tomorrow. Clean his cart."

Evander, I see, is a 200-pound Hampshire boar hog. He's tied front leg and hind to the fence. Mr. Keller must have done that this morning before he left for his mechanic job.

"Get to work," Jeff Tom says. I'd slap him, but he's playing Edward G. Robinson in the movies. I sweep out dust and cob webs, wash the trailer down and spread straw on the floor.

That finished, Jeff Tom says, "Now, scrub Evander." He hands me a long-handled brush. I shrug and splash soapy water on the poor hog. Evander squeals and kicks but stops when the brush caresses his ears and back. It takes two buckets of clear water to rinse away the suds.

"Now, file his hooves."

Jeff Tom looks like a kid who just dropped his ice cream cone.

Filing a hog's hooves is a mystery to me as well. I spent two summers on the Stephens' farm. I slopped hogs and held their legs while they were castrated, but give a beauty treatment? Never.

Then, it occurs to me. Filing a hog's hooves can't be any harder than cutting an orphan boy's toe nails after his first hot bath. I've done that plenty.

I grab the blacksmith's rasp from the fence post, straddle Evander, facing backwards, lift his right rear hoof and file. He lunges and jerks, but twenty minutes later, all four hooves are manicured.

I'm ready for a break, but Jeff Tom hands me a bottle of black shoe polish.

"Dab this on his hooves."

"You're kidding."

"It'll make 'em shine."

"What the hell?"

Shoe polish splatters my jeans and arms, but when I'm finished, Evander looks sharp. The thick black hair across his shoulders glows, the white bristles on his belly gleam, his skin is pink and, of course, his hooves shine black.

"Get him into the smokehouse," Jeff Tom says.

I push, pull, yank and tug, until Evander's inside. Jeff Tom pours slop into a trough and locks the door. Poor hog. He has no mud to roll in and get ugly as he'd like.

* * *

Under the trees, gnats swarm in the hot air and sweat bees attack arms and face. I need a breather. And answers. *Where are the tools kept? Do I have to go to church every*

Sunday? Is there a swimming hole nearby? What half day do I get off work?

Jeff Tom, says, "Stop lollygaggin'. Load that wheelbarrow by the garage with flagstones and push it up to the yard. Daddy limed the grass you're to take out, so he lay a concrete sidewalk this week end. Do as I say, Orphan."

I turn to wring his skinny neck, when Mrs. Keller comes up. She hands me a paper sack. "Your lunch."

To Jeff Tom she goes, "Your plate is on the front porch, dear. A nice breeze there. After lunch, rest a while." Like many parents, Mrs. Keller believes afternoon naps protects her precious Jeff Tom from polio.

She gives me a list of chores. "My goodness, Arthur, don't look so glum. The Lord loves a cheerful worker."

Maybe so. But with only a baloney sandwich, a cup of warm tea and applesauce for dinner, I'll be a damned skinny one.

* * *

I'd hoped to spend another summer with Mr. Stephens and his wife, Rhoda, but that's not to be. Mr. Stephens taught me to dig post holes, cut brush, bale and stack hay, even milk cows. He made hard work, tolerable, if not fun.

He'd smile when I'd forget the nails after I'd climbed onto the roof to replace shingles or laugh and shrug when I'd chip my axe while cutting brush. "It's not a mistake if you learn from it," he'd say.

When the afternoon sun seemed to melt me like a candle, and the hay rake heavy in my hands, he'd toss me a peppermint candy. "This'll spark you up."

What I liked the most though, was when evening shadows lengthened, we'd stow our tools, and Mr. Stephens would slap my shoulder. "Time for a dip, Mr. Arthur."

We'd dive into the cold spring-fed pond and swim while stars twinkled in the evening sky, then join Mrs. Stephens on the cool porch to gorge on thick noodles simmered in tomatoes and onions and covered with thin-sliced steak, sopping up the juices with oven-fresh bread.

"Eat hearty, Mr. Arthur," she'd say, "Eat hearty."

Sundays, after church, Mr. Stephens would drive us forty miles, round trip, in his black Chevy coupe to the "Y" in Sedalia. At the outdoor pool there, he'd swim fifty laps, then toss his car keys into the water. When they settled to the bottom, I'd dive down, pick them up and swim back to him. He'd move farther away with each toss. After three visits, I could swim the length of the pool, under water. Last year, I matched him stroke-for-stroke, lap-for-lap when we swam.

"Swimming every day keeps you young. I'm in my eighties and I out-work men half my age."

* * *

His note arrived in January. Written in black ink on thick paper, each letter formed with curlicues and flourishes, I needed help from Mrs Cave, to decipher it.

I write to say that with great regret I must rescind my invitation for you to lend your labor to my farm this growing season. With a heavy heart, I must report my beloved companion of fifty-seven years, my lovely Rhoda, has departed this mortal realm. I am lonely for her smile. My aching bones and heavy heart are why I've taken residence in town, therefore I have no need for your considerable skills. I regret any disruption to your schedule this may necessitate. The gods are fick-

le. Hence, we may someday break bread together once again.. Remember to swim every day, Mr. Arther. In eternal friendship, I remain.....

Mr. Stephens signed his name in big letters. He understood the ways of the orphanage. He glued a small envelope to his thick stationery. Inside, was a five-dollar bill. If he'd put it in the letter the mail lady would be bucks up and I'd never know of his gift.

With his money and three ones I'd earned selling pop bottles and helping a teacher with Spring Cleaning, maybe I'll have enough cash to buy the radio I've dreamed of since I saw it in the pawn shop window on our annual Orphan's Day field trip. It's worth a try.

* * *

A skill you learn at the Home is how to sneak. At Roll Call, the morning after Mr. Stephens' letter, my money in a Bull Durham tobacco sack hanging down my back, I yell, "Here," when my name's called, slap on the silly white KP hat, tie on an apron, and stroll into the kitchen like that's my work assignment. I grab a garbage can, go down the back steps, empty the can in the incinerator, duck into the grape arbor, slip under the woven wire fence, crawl through the culvert into a ditch, wiggle past a tall hedge to the street, then jump up and run like I'm stealing second base to the bus stop.

When the Grand Avenue bus pulls up, I hop on, drop a nickel in the fare box and slump in my seat. Three blocks from Downtown Pawn and Jewelry, I jump off, my heart beating so loud I'm sure other riders can hear it. I run to the shop. *Is my radio still there? It is!*

I fork over the $7.50 the clerk asks for and carry my

prize back to the Home, careful as if it were a baby kitten. It's Afternoon Prayer time when I creep up the back stairs. I dart from bunk-to-bunk, slide under my bed, open my footlocker quiet as leaves falling, and snuggle my wonderful radio inside.

The boy's Rest Room smells like Pinesol and Bon Ami. I open a stall and stand on the stool. Ole Man Tutt calls, "Anyone in here?"

I give a fake sneeze. He hears this and opens the stall door. When he sees it's me, he smiles, happy he saved a sinner from the fires of Hell. He promises me a swat with the pine paddle and pins the No Cookie Privileges card to my shirt. If Brother Seymour had caught me, I'd have been sentenced to 2 days isolation, minimum.

That night, it seems the Free Time bell will never ring. Before it stops jangling, I'm at my locker. Then, I set the most beautiful radio in the world on my pillow. I dial in KMOX. I dance when I hear the Cardinals' famous announcer say, "Hello, everybody. Harry Caray here, coming to you from beautiful Sportsman Park in St. Louis, where the Cardinals play the Boston Braves under the lights tonight."

Every Cardinal game from that night until I left for slave duty, my bunk is crowded with kids, all eager to hear Harry's famous home run call: "Its way, way back there. It might be. It could be. It is! A home run. Holy Cow!"

Before catching the bus for Wheatland, I wrapped my precious radio in a towel, buttoned my spare jeans around it, and placed it tenderly in my suitcase, so it will ride safely. My key to survival this summer.

* * *

When I learned Mrs. Stephens had passed, I blinked back tears. Quick as a rabbit, with a laugh that tinkled like a door bell, she'd bring me raisin cookies every night before sack time. She said she was thirteen when she married Mr. Stephens on a Greek island before they came to America. Her most prized wedding gift was a white sheepskin rug. My first night she spread it on the floor beside my bed.

"You deserve the best, Mr. Arthur. Our ancient folk tales recount the lives of many orphans. Dionysus was one. He became a God. Those with big souls always get big rewards."

Mornings when Mr. Stephens and I'd leave for the fields, she'd stand beside the door. Mr. Stephens would ask, "Where's my kiss, Woman?" She'd laugh and press her mouth against his. My throat aches remembering her smile and gentle gray eyes.

* * *

Now, in a different world and different time, Mrs. Keller calls, "Supper."

I bounce up the steps ready to do serious damage to a home-cooked meal. Mrs. Keller stops me at the kitchen door.

"Your plate's in the wash house, Arthur. That's where you'll take your meals from now on."

She points to a small building off the back porch. "Be sure to pray. Thank God for His many blessings."

I've been quarantined, huh? Does she really think I can infect Jeff Tom, so he'll be an orphan? Or, is it that she thinks she's too good to share meals with a dumb orphan? Whatever the reason, I pray again this is my last year as a summer slave.

* * *

The laundry room smells of damp concrete, wet wool and vinegar. A Maytag ringer washing machine stands next to two empty wash tubs. My plate is on a card table beside a two-burner hot plate, a small cooking pan on one burner, and a box of Faultless Starch on the table. A single yellow light-bulb dangles from the ceiling.

I'd like to spit in Mrs. Keller's face. She should've told me sooner where I'd eat, not pop it on me just as I'm ready to sit down. Kids from the Home talk about this.

"When it happens, smile and say, 'Jesus loves you.' That'll piss 'em off. Who cares where you eat, as long as you do?"

I gobble my food, rinse my dishes at the kitchen sink, mumble thank you and bolt outside. I could eat cardboard. Two pieces of bacon, a spoon of cold cabbage, a square of red Jell-O and glass of purple Kool-Aid is poor reward for the work I did today.

The cattle trough is filled with clean water. I plunge my aching hands in it up to my elbows, to take the sting from my blisters. *Someday, I'll eat what I want, where I want, when I want. And get paid lots of money for the work I do. Please, God, make this my last year as slave labor. Please.*

I'm sunburned and tired. *If I hit the hay now, maybe I can catch a few innings of the Cardinals' game. After that, it'll be my buddy, John McCormack.*

* * *

At the Home, when night noises fill the dorm, a towel wrapped around my radio, the volume low, my ear close to the dial, I listen: "John McCormack, here. The Man Who Walks and Talks at Midnight. The man, the broadcasting man, coming to you over 50,000 red-hot, clear channel watts from KMOX, the voice of St.Louis."

McCormack's not just a disc jockey, though he plays records. He's an educator. He introduces Bing Crosby with,

"Harry Lillis Crosby was born in Tacoma, Washington, on May 3rd, 1903, in the house his father built. Here's Bing, with the state song of Kansas, 'Home on the Range'."

Before Rosemary Clooney sings, "Here's the pride and joy of Maysville, Kentucky. Joe and Marie Clooney's little girl, Rosemary, and her great hit, 'Come On-a My House.'"

McCormack reports who Mickey Rooney married this time and says Clark Gable seeks happiness from other women after the death of his true love, Carole Lombard. McCormack's weather reports are geography lessons.

"In Rome, the Eternal City, it's clear and 70 degrees. In Paris, the City of Lights, it's 67, a light rain kissing the Notre Dame Cathedral." *Someday, somehow, I'll visit the wonderful places he talks about.*

I sleep some and listen some, but I'm all ears when Mr. McCormack signs off at 6 a.m., with the Mormon Tabernacle Choir singing, "The Lord's Prayer." When the words, "The kingdom and the power and the glory forever, amen," float out, I stow my nighttime companion carefully in my footlocker and go help the little ones get ready for the day.

* * *

Now, in Wheatland, Missouri, after a hard day's work, my hands up to my elbows in a water trough, Mr. Keller comes up. He wears khaki pants and a green, army tee shirt.

"Sore hands, huh? After all ya done today, I reckon so. Figured it'd take two days to clean them coops. Ya did it in a mornin'."

A goldfish flashes orange in the water trough.

Mr. Keller keeps talking. "Last year's orphan was worthless. Mrs. Keller says she spent more time wipin' his nose than he did workin'. I was in the Army. Motor pool.

Anyone can kill Krauts, but it takes smarts to keep jeeps and trucks runnin'."

I don't say the war's been over six years, or that ducking bullets is more dangerous than changing spark plugs.

Mr. Keller grins. "Took yer shirt off this mornin', huh? Can't blame ya. Mrs. Keller's never worked under a tin roof with a hot sun bearin' down."

He picks up a thick maple limb, pulls a silver knife from his front pocket, flicks his wrist, and cuts it in two. He peels bark off the longest piece. "Need a new switch for Jeff Tom."

He holds up his knife. "Best tool ever. Use it mebbe ten times a day." He drops it into his pocket again.

"When yer chores are done and Mrs. Keller says it's okay, grab a pole from the garage and go fishin'. Wild Horse River has some good holes. I've caught some biggun's just past the bridge at Twin Rocks, 'fore Devil's Falls. By the way, Mrs. Keller washes yer goods ever other Monday. Drop yer duds in the basket agin the wall where ya eat."

The gold fish floats to the surface its mouth cutting circles in the water. I flick my finger. He darts for safety in the dark water at the trough's bottom.

The anger I had toward Jeff Tom, Mrs. Keller, the skimpy supper, and my washroom dining hall fades. I built the gallows and put the noose around my own neck when I didn't get the rules straight this morning. Mr. Keller seems like a straight shooter.

His jaw muscles dance. "'Bout Fatima.' She ain't Evelyn's favorite. Me? I like her. She works hard. Minds her two brothers. Cooks. Totes water."

He smiles and clicks his tongue. "Shore fills out a pair of shorts, don't she? But, San Quintin Quail gets ya twenty, my friend, so keep yer pants zipped."

I nod.

"'Bout yer eatin' arrangements. Mrs. Keller thinks help oughta eat separate from family."

I don't say anything. To me, Mrs. Keller sentenced me to eat alone in the wash house because she thinks that's good enough for orphans. I glance toward the smoke house.

Mr. Keller says, "Sack time, huh? Fine. Startin' 'morrow mornin' let's go over yer chores for the day 'fore I leave. Okay?"

I nod. *Who do the Cards play? The Dodgers?*

The muscle in Mr. Keller's jaw works again. "'Bout Jeff Tom. He's just a boy. Be patient, okay?" He lays the switch he just made on a fence post. "That a radio I seen in yer gear? Get it hooked up all right?"

I nod, drying my hands on my jeans.

He sticks his hand out. We shake. I head for bed. Tomorrow's another day.

* * *

"Tears don't care where they fall," Fatima says.

We're in a tree house in the big elm. A broken moon hangs in the eastern sky. A breeze stirs the leaves.

"This is my Secret Place, Orphan Boy." She breathes deep. "What happened to your parents?"

I'm ready this time. "Dad killed more Japs than Audie Murphy did Krauts. He knocked out Ezzard Charles and Jersey Joe Walcott on the same night to become heavyweight champ. Mom's a movie star. I bought an Orphanage 'cause I like to beat up on kids."

She doesn't laugh. "Be a smart aleck. See if I care."

The truth is, Dwayne came home from the third grade

and found me asleep in my snow suit on the divan. A can of Carnation milk and loaf of bread was on the table next to an ashtray. Momma was gone.

We ate the bread and drank the milk.

When Momma didn't show after 3 days, Dwayne took us to a store where I begged for a sandwich and a Payday Candy Bar. The store owner called the cops. They took us to the Home. A few days later, a policeman came and showed Dwayne pictures of a dead woman. Dwayne said it was Momma. The cop told Brother Seymour a sailor killed her.

Later, Dwayne said he lied, that it wasn't Momma in the pictures, that she worked at Kresge's and Dad was killed in the Battle of the Bulge, and before he shipped out, he bought a black Cadillac and if I wasn't so damn dumb I'd remember riding all over town in it. Dwayne says Momma wears a mink coat and has blonde hair.

I remember a lady who smelled like cigarettes slapping me when I couldn't stop coughing. Dwayne says I have an over-active imagination, that Momma will come for us soon.

I'm still waiting.

Fatima goes, "Mami speaks Spanish and un poco English. Papi nada Spanish. We lived in Phoenix before moving here. Papi told Paul, Joanna's husband, get a job or get out. My little brother, Juan's retarded. Jaime's just stubborn."

She takes a big breath. "Why weren't you adopted?"

I go straight this time. "I was. Almost, anyway. Twice. The Rentschler's only had to sign the papers. Then a hay baler tore off Cliff's arm. I was eight. Momma Agnes brought me back to the Home because Cliff had to stay in the hospital a long time and they ran out of money."

"Too bad. The other time?"

"The Whittaker's. I was there from almost ten to

twelve. They owned a restaurant. I ate hamburgers and drank milk shakes every day. Momma Kay got mad when she found Les had a secret girlfriend. They divorced. Momma Kay said she'd adopt me when things settled down."

One Christmas, she came for me. Brought me a Lone Ranger pistol and holster and bag of candy corn. Brother Seymour won't let me leave with her that night, so Momma Kay threw a paper weight at him."

The facility manager walked her to the bus. They locked me in a room upstairs. I crawled out a window and shimmed down the drain pipe looking for her."

I skip the part where I spend two days in a coal shed before a nice lady finds me, cleans me up, and feeds me tomato soup. She and her husband walk me back to the Home, the lady crying all the way.

Brother Seymour gave me twenty whacks with the pine paddle and locked me in the Rubber Room. I screamed 'til I couldn't talk. It was three weeks before they let me rejoin general population.

Fatima goes, "I'd like to be adopted. A pretty lady who'd let me wear lipstick and mascara. And read Modern Romance. We'd go to picture shows. Lots of 'em."

The wind sways the tree. I say, "Dwayne was Squad Bay Captain when I came back from the Whittaker's. At morning milk, he'd skip me. When I won the Dorm Spelling Bee, he slapped me 'til my nose bled. 'You're not so smart, Fart Face, or you'd have stayed gone.'"

I don't mention that after Dwayne made starting quarterback, he'd come to my bunk and we'd wrestle. Sometimes, he'd hold me down and loop a belt around my throat so tight I couldn't breathe. "You're a worthless dick, just like Dad."

The next day he'd give me so many cookies I'd sell

'em two for a penny and pocket a dime. During the All-City Championship game, Dwayne fumbled once and threw two interceptions. Brother Seymour expelled him.

I do tell Fatima, "Dwayne's in the Army. I'll enlist when I graduate. I used to hope we'd be in the same outfit, but I don't know where he's stationed. He sent me a post card with a picture of a grasshopper big as a cow on it. The farmer's holding a milk bucket. The caption read, "Is my bucket big enough?"

Dwayne wrote on the card, 'They grow them big here. Stay in school.' The postmark was so smeared not even Mrs. Cave could tell where it was mailed from."

We listen to the wind. A house dog barks off to the west. Fatima breathes deep. "Joanna's big as a water tower. I don't want to be p.g. like her. She's just fourteen months older than me. Paul and her went to visit his sick momma. I like that they're gone. I can walk without stumbling over feet."

She sits up. "You like Mr. Keller?"

"He's all right, I guess."

"Gives me the willies. Followed me one night. I swung up here and pulled up the rope before he saw me. He kept calling, 'Pretty Fatima, you won two dollars.Come get it.' Scared the breath outta me. After a while he went to the house. When he and Mrs. Keller yelled at each other, I ran home. Fast."

"Wasn't he worried Mrs. Keller would hear him?'

"Maybe she did. Who knows. Mami says, 'A dirty rag never wipes clean.' Mrs.Keller has problems of her own."

Fatima slaps my leg."Whatcha wanna be when you grow up?"

"Ball player. Cardinals. Second base. You?"

"Singer. A band played at the VFW Club. Me and Momma got in free because we cleaned up after the show.

Their girl singer can't sing as good as I can. She just knows more songs. I don't have a radio to learn from."

"I do."

"A radio? Really? Can I listen to it?"

"Any time."

* * *

I left Mr. Keller at the water trough and went to my cot in the smoke house. I'd plugged my radio into the overhead light socket that morning, but static was so bad I snapped it off. My room was hot as a broom closet.

Where could I cool off? Wasn't that an elm I saw in the far pasture? Up high, there'll be a breeze.

Outside, bats wheel in the starry sky. Whippoorwills call. The mosquitoes aren't out, yet. Brownie, the Keller's milk cow, chumps on her cud beneath the elm. I pat her damp side. A rope bumps my head. Even in the dark, I make out wood strips nailed to the tree trunk. I grab the rope, step on a slat and swing into the tree bough, easy as taking off my shirt.

Boards are wedged into the bough to make a platform. From here, the whole world stretches out in all direction. To the east, the Wild Horse River glints in the moonlight. Below, the Keller's house is small as a cigar box. Fatima's trailer just a grey shadow. To the west, the veterinarian's barn and silo are toys in the moonlight, cattle grazing in the pasture dark dots.

A door slams. A man yells, "That's a lot of money, dammit." A woman answers in Spanish. Minutes later, the rope moves. Fatima swings up beside me.

"Scared the snot outta me, Orphan Boy. How'd you find this?"

"'Bout hung myself on your rope."

"My Secret Place. Good, huh?"

"Yeah."

This was before we talked about my being an orphan and I said I had a radio. Now, storm clouds cover the moon. Lightening splits the sky. Thunder booms.

"It's gonna rain pitch forks," Fatima says. "Let's listen to your radio."

"Aw right. John McCormack's on."

"Who?"

"The world's best radio man. C'mon."

We swing down. The rain hits us in the barnyard. We burst through the door into my room, soaked but cooled off. I yank on the light and toss Fatima my towel.

My heart stops. Where's my radio? I should be on the chest of drawers. It's gone. I open the top drawer. Empty. As are the other two drawers. What I care about the most in the world has disappeared. *I'm gonna puke.*

Faima watches. I yank the chest away from the wall. No radio. I can hardly breathe. *Where is my lifeline?*

Fatima snorts. "Why are you acting like you lost something? You don't have a radio. You lied to get me alone. Grow up, Orphan Boy." She's out the door.

I yell, "Fatima, don't go. You'll get wet."

Stupid, Carr.

My beautiful Phillips was fhere when I left for the tree house. Now, it's gone. *Jeff Tom stole it. I'll wring your neck, you thieving little shit. I have other plans for Fatima.*

* * *

Morning breaks hot and clear. I eat cereal in the laundry room. Mrs. Keller comes in with my list of chores.

"Mr. Keller was called to work early," she says. "The

storm flooded his place of employment. He'll work late tonight, I'm afraid. A Christian neighbor will carry Jeff Tom and Evander to the fair." She leaves me to soggy corn flacks and warm milk.

I eat with an eye on the kitchen, in case Jeff Tom shows. He doesn't. I rinse my bowl and spoon and run to the pig pen. Evander grunts and snorts, his cart hooked to a pickup truck. Two sheep and a crate of chickens fill the truck bed. Jeff Tom stands next to the cab.

I go, "Hey, man. Glad I caught you. What chores do you want done, while you're gone?"

He follows me into the smoke house. I slam him against the wall. "You fucking thief! Where's my radio?"

"Radio? What radio?" His blue eyes go wide. He's just a baby. I hate what I have to do, but kids are great thieves. And liars.

Jeff Tom says, "Let go." He pulls at my hands.

My mouth next to his ear, I say, "Where. Is. It?"

"You're crazy, man. Momma don't let radios on her property. Maybe them Mexicans stole it. Daddy say they'll steal wash off their momma's clothes line."

Somehow, I believe the little turd didn't steal my radio. I shove him away.

He rubs his throat. "I won't tell Momma."

Outside, Mrs. Keller is near the door. "Hurry, darling. Good deeds should be rewarded with diligence. Mr. Griffin's waiting." Jeff Tom runs for the pickup.

Mrs. Keller asks, "Arthur, were you and Jeff Tom speaking of a radio?"

"Yes, ma'am."

"What about it?"

"Mine was stolen."

"That's a most serious accusation, Arthur. You've just misplaced it."

"It was on the dresser last night. Now, it's gone."

Her eyes search mine. "It'll re-surface, I'm sure. Now, we've work to do."

For her, this topic is dead. For me, it's very much alive.

* * *

It's a busy morning. First, Brownie needs milking, since Mr. Keller went to work early and left this chore for me. Tomato plants need re-staking after last night's storm. There are green beans to pick, cabbage to weed, canning jars brought in from the garage, so Mrs. Keller can put up the beans. Then I push two wheelbarrow loads of flagstones into the yard, and begin ripping up grass, so Mr. Keller can lay his side walk.

Lunch is a peanut butter and jelly sandwich, a too-ripe apple and purple Kool-Aid, eaten under the maples next to the water trough. When I start work after a privy call Mrs. Keller comes up.

"Where were you? I've been waiting. Wise workers use their time expeditiously." She shakes a long finger at me. "Here's an immediate assignment. Tree limbs were blown onto the roof last night. Get a ladder from the garage and clear them off."

On the roof, the limbs lay near an upstairs window. I belly out, grab a branch and lift. It catches on a shingle. *If I crawl out further, I can lift the limb, and heave it into the yard below.* It crashes to the ground. Organ music plays.

From a radio? I listen closely. More music floats by, then it's only sparrows squabbling in the trees beside the house.

Aha. Maybe Jeff Tom did steal my night -time companion. But, he's at the fair. Did someone at the veterinarian's house play the organ and the sound drifted over here?

I listen a minute more. When I hear nothing, I climb down, stow the ladder, chop up the limbs, carry them to the compost pile, and return to busting sod. Mrs. Keller comes up.

"I see you removed the limbs successfully." She shields her pale blue eyes with a thin white hand. "Our annual livestock fair starts this very evening. After your chores are finished, if you so desire, you may attend. You ride a bicycle, I assume?"

"Yes, ma'am."

"Santa Claus brought Jeff Tom a Swinn. He's been dilatory in learning to ride it. If you're careful, you may use it for the evening. But, I caution you, the smallest scratch will break his heart."

"I understand, ma'am." I'm surprised she mentioned Santa Claus and bicycle. I didn't know she had any fun in her.

"It's an easy ride. Follow the road over the Wild Horse River Bridge, turn right at the water tower. You'll see it."

She doesn't mention my missing radio. I've woolled it's disappearance over in my mind all day and keep coming back to Jeff Tom. He stole so he can listen to, "Tom Mix," "Sky King" and the "B-Bar-B Riders." *When I get him alone, I'll slap him 'til he fesses up.*

* * *

Mrs. Keller is right. It's an easy ride to the Fairgrounds. I hide Jeff Tom's bike in the weeds and get my bearings. Before I climbed on the bus in St. Louis three days ago, I hid four one-dollar bills in my underwear, money I'd earned washing windows and helping a teacher plant her garden. I take out a dollar, go into the café, order two hot dogs and a Grapette, then find a seat in the grandstand to watch the hog show.

Local folks pile into the stands, greeting each other with back slaps and handshakes. Jeff Tom and a girl with a gob of red hair, herd their hogs into the ring. The show judge looks both Hampshires over carefully. *Farmers around here must raise Durocs or Chester Whites, since there only two Hampshires on display.*

Imogene Hobbs wins a Best Hampshire sow, blue ribbon. Jeff Tom and Evander are awarded Best Hampshire, Boar and Best in Show.

Jeff Tom is all smiles when he leads Evander back to his pen. I follow.

"Congratulations, Thief. Whoop-de-do."

"No radio, huh?" He faces me. "You're bigger than me. Touch me again, and I'll tell Daddy. You'll be sorry then."

So, he's gonna bring out the heavy artillery? I don't have a parent to tattle to.

Jeff Tom says, "If I stole your silly radio, Momma'd find it and tell Daddy. He'd blister my ass. He gets crazy when he's riled. He'd beat you up. Me. Momma. Anybody."

The Little Shit's eyes tell me he's not my thief.

Jeff Tom goes, "The vet's office across the road was broken into the other night. Maybe that's who got your radio."

He edges toward the gate. "I want Momma to see my ribbons." Outside the pen, he turns. "What I said about Daddy? That's between us. Okay?"

Have it your way, Asshole.

* * *

A man, wearing a white apron comes up. "Had my eye on ya. Yer Keller's orphan?"

"Yes, sir."

"Bob Sheets." He extends his hand. "Me and my wife run the café here. My regular help fell out of a tree and broke his foot. Can't work. Wanna make a buck?"

"Yes, sir."

"Good. You're hired." He slaps my shoulder. "My Momma raised three boys. Alone. Know the road yer travellin'."

He gestures toward the café. "Keller's in the bar if ya need his permission. Said earlier ya was a hard worker."

I'm taken aback. I thought Keller was working late. Instead, he's sucking suds in a bar. I don't need his permission to work on my own time.

"Where's my apron?"

"Back wall. We'll settle up at closin' time."

* * *

I'm clearing tables when a man everybody calls Uncle Elias, waves me over, his stool next to Keller's. "This boy's no runt like last year's orphan, Ralph."

Mr. Keller eyes me good. *I'm glad I washed up before I pedaled into town.*

"Evelyn went easy on ya today, huh? I'd been there, ya'd be too tired to piss, much less work extra."

Uncle Elias goes, "What happened to your folks, boy?"

I'm ready. "Dad's an Army general. He's teaching Japs democracy. General Douglas MacArthur. You've probably heard of him. Mom's starring on Broadway. . ."

"Okay, okay. Had that coming. Not many orphans 'round here. When the Mexican invasion starts, we'll have plenty of little brown bastards. They're worse."

He slaps my arm. "Ain't you old enough to be cannon fodder for Harry Truman's army?"

"I'll register when I'm eighteen," I say, and head for the kitchen.

Wilma Sheets is the waitress. She said, "You're my pig tail." I know what a pig tail is from my time with the Whittaker's, who ran a restaurant. They fill water glasses, make milkshakes, buss tables, fill coffee cups and do side work so the waitress can take orders and serve food.

We're busy. I'm wiping down Station 3 when Fatima and her date, Tony Aguilera, come in. Fatima sits while Tony jaws with Wilma. He wears a white undershirt with no sleeves, tan slacks and black belt. His moustache is thin and black, his hair slicked back.

I pour water for Fatima. "He win you a kewpie doll?"

"Find your radio, Orphan Boy?"

Her smile makes my throat ache. Her black hair is tied with a white bow. Her lips are red. She wears a white blouse with black buttons down the front, a black skirt with white pockets, and a wide red belt. Her black and white high heels make her look taller and older.

She nods toward Tony. "He's got Roman hands and Russian fingers. Think a cheeseburger with double onions will slow him down?"

Mr. Keller staggers up. "How's my pretty tenant girl? Ya dress up jist for me? Give me a kiss."

Fatima leans back. "Hello, Mr. Keller. Evelyn here? I'd like to tell her of the delightful game you invented the other night. The one where you said you had two dollars for me?"

"Nobody'll believe ya, even if it did happen." He grabs

her shoulder. "Ya need a man, not a boy."

Tony Aguilera rushes up. "She's my date, Old Man. Move on, or I'll knock yer block off."

"Ya got a big mouth for a scrawny-assed Mexican."

"Wanna go outside? Or die here?" Tony's hand is in his pocket.

Mr. Keller says, "Pull that knife and it's the last thing you do. I was in the army, Spic."

Uncle Elias comes up and grabs Mr. Keller's arm. "Ralph, behave yourself. You ain't Gorgeous George." Uncle Elias must watch wrestling on television.

Bob Sheets hurries up with a baseball bat.

"Trouble's over, Bob," Uncle Elias says. "Ralph's goin' home. Save your licks for a ball game."

Mr. Keller peeks around Uncle Elias. "That Studebaker outside yours, Brown Boy?"

"What's it to you?"

"Got brake troubles?"

"Never."

"I guarantee ya will. I'm a mechanic. I know."

Uncle Elias says, "C'mon on. Ralph. Let's go. Alex'll drive my truck. You stay out any later and Evelyn'll snatch you baldheaded." He kinda pulls Mr. Keller toward the door.

Customers mill at the front entrance, wanting service. Bob Sheets says, "Sorry folks. We're closed. I'm outta beef and buns. Sorry." Folks grumble but shuffle off.

Bob Sheets says, "Art, empty the trash and we'll settle up. That Mexican girl's a real looker. She cause the ruckus?"

"No sir. Ralph Keller. Wanted to drag race her date." I figure that's all he needs to know.

"Ralph's belligerent as hell when he drinks."

I take the trash to the burn barrel across the parking

lot. I hear Uncle Elias' voice. "Ralph Keller, what the hell you doin' on the ground?"

Mr. Keller says, "Checkin' out a certain Spic's brakes. In case they go out later." He slips something shiny into his front pocket as he stands.

Uncle Elias says, "Let's get you home 'fore you inspect ever car in the lot." They drive off. Alex follows in Uncle Elias' pickup.

I stow the empty trash cans, get Jeff Tom's bike from the weeds and go to the kitchen. Bob Sheets hands me a buck. "'Preciate your help."

Wilma flips me a quarter. "Me, too. You're good."

I thank them. *Kitchen Practice at the Home paid off. Finally.*

Bob Sheets follows me outside. "No bike light? Ya'll get run over. Can't have that. I need ya. Five o'clock tomorrow. Okay?

"You bet."

"I'll strap my frog light on yer handle bar."

Five minutes later, with Bob Sheets' hunting lamp killing the shadows, I ride across the gravel parking lot. Tony Aguilar and Fatima are in his car, windows rolled down. Fatima says, "Don't. It's our first date. Your radio work?"

I can't hear Tony, but Fatima says, "So I can sing along."

She can listen to my radio. Anytime. Then, I remember. I don't have one. It was stolen.

* * *

The night air is soft, with a half-moon and a million stars. A car passes going so fast I can't see what make it is. At the Wild Horse Bridge, it fish tails. Rocks shoot into the night.

Sparks dance. The car slams into the bridge railing, goes airborne and plunges into the river below.

It takes me a second or two to digest what I just saw, then I pedal fast for the bridge. I drag Jeff Tom's bike down a fisherman's path to a clearing on the bank. The only sign the river just swallowed a car, are small ripples in the black water.

I shuck my clothes, except underwear and tennis shoes, set Bob's light on a rock and wade out. The water's cold from last night's rain. *Watch for sunken logs, Carr.*

I breast stroke out to where the smell of gas and oil is strongest, and dive. Eight or ten feet down, I feel metal and glass. *Passenger door. Gone.* A shoe floats past. I grab it and surface. In the moonlight, I see it's a black and white high heel. Fatima's.

I flip the shoe to the bank, take a deep breath, and use a willow sapling to pull myself down. I feel under the dash board. A body. One jerk and it floats free. Using a lifeguard's hold, I swim for shore with the corpse.

I'm in shallow water when two fishermen run up. "Did a fuckin' car go off the bridge? That a body?" This from a boy waving a lantern.

A man with a carbide light on his cap wades out to help me pull Tony Aguilera's body onto the bank. Tony's head is split open. One side of his moustache is shaved off, neat as a razor cut.

"Call the sheriff. Ambulance!" I yell.

The boy goes, "No telephone."

"Stop a car!"

"He's dead. Why worry?"

The older fisherman goes, "Dammit, Audie. Do as yer told."

Where's Fatima? I swim out to the sapling and pull

myself down. The front and back seat cushions float against the car's roof. *She's not there. Was she thrown out when the door came off?*

Three strokes and a kick takes me to the water grass and saplings along the far bank. *Maybe she floated over here.*

The old man's light finds me. "Lookin' for a body?"

"Yeah. A girl's."

"Current'll carry it over the falls, probably."

I remember Fatima mentioned Devil's Falls and Twin Rocks. Two boulders rise from the river, black as Angus bulls. Behind them, darkness and the roar of falling water.

Something catches my eye. I swim closer. A log pile. My eyes search it. I see a flash of white. *Fatima?*

Up close it's a cottonwood limb with bark scrapped away. My arms are heavy. *Give it up Carr. Get out. Search on foot. The old fisherman will help.*

The log raft rotates. Something dark hangs inches above the water. Fatima! A nasty gash runs from forehead to chin. Her hands are cold. She groans at my touch.

"Hang on. I'll get you out of here."

She whispers, "That you, Orphan Boy?"

I put my left arm under her chin, and swim, but she doesn't come. She's snagged. I dive under. A tree limb has grabbed her skirt. I surface. The raft spins faster. Mist is thick here. *Get a plan, Carr, fast. Or, die.*

I dive to untangle Fatima's skirt. My fingers don't work right. I surface. My arms are numb. I've read about this. *What'd they call it? Hyperthermia? My only chance is get the raft into shallow water.*

I recall what Mr. Stephens said. "Your legs are your strongest asset in water. Use 'em."

I put my shoulder against the raft and kick. Hard. Then

harder. The raft stops spinning. I kick more, hoping to guide it into shallow water. A boulder, big as a pickup truck, juts up to my right, forming an eddy. *Where's shallow water?*

I kick more, inching the logs forward. Then, the raft rises in one motion and goes airborne. I wrap my arms around a log. The raft slams me onto a sand bar. I cough silt and leaves, then stagger to my feet. The water's chest deep. The raft landed against a rock shelf. Fatima dangles in the water. I splash over to her.

"We're safe," I say.

Not true, Carr. She has to be un-hooked. Carried to the road. Somehow you have to get her to a hospital.

I hear the pop-pop of a motor boat. I yell, "Over here!" A voice answers. "Boy, where are ya?"

It's the old fisherman. I shout and wave, though that's stupid. An hour seems to pass before his boat glides up.

I babble. "A limbs got her."

"I'll get under it. Cut her down." He hands me his knife.

My hands shake, but his Barlow slices the wet cloth, and I lower Fatima into the boat, then pull myself in beside her.

The fisherman says, "Ya got them logs to shore jist in time. Another thirty feet ya'd be a goner." He's all business. "Raincoat's hers. Tarp yours. I only got a two-and-a-half-horse Merc, but it'll get us there."

It must have, because I next remember standing by an ambulance, hugging a blanket, coffee cup in hand. A silly question crosses my mind. *Did the Cards win today?*

"We'll get her to the hospital," a man in rubber gloves and white coat says. "Broke ribs. Internal organs busted, I 'spec. She'll probably lose a leg."

The sheriff says, "From skid marks on the bridge looks like brakes on the car went out. We'll never know. It was smashed to shit goin' over the falls."

He slaps my back. "Ya saved us time and money draggin' that Mexican out of the water."

I don't tell him I saw Ralph Keller on the ground beside Tony's car at Bob Sheets' cafe. When Ralph stood, he stuffed what I'm sure was his knife, into his pocket and told Uncle Elias he was inspecting Tony's brakes. I think he cut Tony's brake line, but it would be an orphan's word against a supposed war hero. Any fool knows who they'd believe.

Besides, I have no real proof, just a hunch. That I kept a Mexican girl from going over the falls might be reason enough to not believe one word I'd say.

* * *

I'm at the Keller's. My radio on the chest of drawers. Mrs. Keller and Jeff Tom stand in the doorway. "Sheriff says you saved Fatima's life." Her hands work at her apron hem. "Found your radio where you left it."

She moves closer. "Took it to my room to protect it from the elements. Listened to two programs. Too much music and not enough Gospel for me." Her voice almost a whisper, "It's lonesome when my men are gone."

I can't believe what I hear. Then, I remember Fatima said a dirty rag never wipes clean. To Mrs. Keller, the truth is how she arranges the facts. The Home is filled with people like her. Here's my chance. If I take off now, she won't say a thing, just mail the Home their twenty five bucks each month, like I'm *still there. When I'm due to return in September, she'll buy a bus ticket to St. Louis like normal. If the Trailways pulls in and I'm not on it, and Brother Seymour calls, which he won't, she'll say she watched me to my seat. She has the ticket stub as proof.*

Jeff Tom says, "See? I didn't steal yer radio."

In her little girl voice Mrs. Keller says, "Ralph Keller's a good provider. Like most men, he lacks judgment from time-to-time. Yes, he's partial to drink on rare occasions. Perhaps you'll find it in your heart to forgive his small trespasses?"

Wow. I've got to get out of here. Fast.

Mrs. Keller keeps talking. "From now on, Arthur, you'll eat with us. I even prepared you a comfortable cot on the back porch."

I force a smile. "That's right decent of you, Evelyn, but I'm leaving. Tell the Orphanage what you will. When school's out, I'll join the Army."

* * *

I rented a room from Bob Sheets, enrolled in high school, worked weekends at his restaurant and did odd jobs for spending money. Most nights, I'd listen to my radio. People say everyone knows everything in a small town. Maybe.

I saw Ralph Keller once the entire time. He'd been drinking when he came by the café. He gave me a long stare but didn't speak. With Bob Sheets and his baseball there Keller was probably afraid to say anything. Whatever the reason, that was the last I saw of him.

* * *

The bus leaves for Kansas City and the Military Induction Center in thirty minutes. I have one last visit to make.

I haven't seen Fatima since the night she went off the bridge. When she left the hospital, her folks had moved, so she took a job at the shoe factory and rented a room at Verna Stucky's Boarding Manor.

She answers my knock with a hug. Her nose is lopsided, a scar across her right cheek. "Find your radio, Orphan Boy?"

"Win a Kewpie Doll, Girl?"

We both laugh. I sit.

"Doctors saved my leg, but I'll always limp." Her smile hurts my throat. "I read a lot while in the hospital. One article said most people live in fear. Afraid they'll lose what they now have or won't get what they want. Makes sense. Take Evelyn Keller. She's afraid she'll lose Ralph. And Ralph's scared we'll find out he's not the war hero he wants us to believe he is."

Tears rim her black eyes. "Tony Aguilera? A silly boy afraid to be a man. Sorry, he won't get the chance." She pauses. "Me? I'm afraid folks won't like me." She laughs.

"And you, Art Carr. You're afraid you won't measure up to that invisible yardstick inside that only you can see. But, you sure can swim. Thanks."

I laugh. I'd like to talk longer, but I've a bus to catch.

"Learned any new songs lately?"

"No radio."

I take my beloved Phillips from my bag and hand it to her.

"You do now."

She grins. "So, you did have one, after all. It'll come in handy at my new job. Doctor Rusk's wife wants help with housework and minding her boys." That crooked smile again. "My two brothers taught me how to take care of boys. I'll enroll in night school in the fall."

* * *

Dwayne's on the telephone. "That you, Archer?"

That's how I said my name when little.

"Yeah, Dain. It's me." That's how I said his.

"Mom was transferred. That's why she never came for us." Dwayne's sticking to his story.

I laugh. "You made that lie up to protect me, Dwayne. We both know she's dead."

The line goes silent. "You're grown, huh? Where you callin' from?"

"VA hospital. St. Louis."

"Enlist?"

"Yeah. Sent to Korea. Waltzed with a Chinese potato masher. Lost a leg."

"Goddamn." He says this more than once. Then, "Know why I'm in Leavenworth?"

"Want to tell me?"

"Me and two guys robbed a base exchange. Had three great days. Art, you should've seen the money. I'm pullin' twenty-five. Out in '73. Can you come see me?"

"It'll be a month or so before I'm discharged."

"A real visit, Art. Not like when I said Mom would come."

"Don't worry, Dain. Archer'll be there."

A male voice interrupts. "Inmate Carr's telephone privileges have expired." The line goes dead.

I didn't tell Dwayne that one hot Missouri summer a young lady pulled me though the knothole of manhood and taught me about fear. That was Fatima's miracle.

The End

RIVERS TO CROSS

RIVERS TO CROSS

We park under a big tree where a school once stood says Know-it All Wayne. He hands us hip-high rubber boots. "Bridges have probably washed out," he says. Andy, pulls his on, looks at me and whistles. "Quite a fashion statement, Pretty Girl." I smile. I need that.

The bridge over the Blackwater River sways, but we cross as inky black water swirls around large rocks, sending white mist into the air. Once across, we skirt a cornfield and follow a crooked path up a steep hill.

It seems like hours before we collapse in the shade of tall trees and choke down stale sandwiches bought yesterday in St. Louis. Too soon, we trudge up hill to the Smoke River, where the water runs fast and gray. Wayne cuts a long pole. "We'll have to wade. Grab on, Sam. You too, Andy." Swift water tugs at us as we scramble over sharp rocks, yet no one falls. We crawl up the far bank to a grassy spot.

"How much further," I ask.

"An hour or so."

"Why didn't you tell me we'd climb hills and wade rivers?"

He shrugs. "You said you wanted to see your Daddy's grave. Ya ask about the terrain."

The White River laughs and gurgles in the sun. I splash cool water on my face and neck. "If this is a river, I'm an ice cream cone," I whisper to Andy. He grins and flicks a piece of grass at me. The bridge is out, so we wade shallow water, past slabs of rocks long as a phone booth.

On the other side, Wayne reports like a TV weather man, "Only a mile or so now." *He better be right. My blisters have blisters. Quite a wild goose chase, Sam.*

We weave through cedar trees to a pile of weed-covered logs and rotten lumber. Wayne whispers like he's in church. "All that's left of our cabin."

I say to Andy, "It sure was tiny."

"But a mansion to those who lived here."

Wayne finds a big rock and wipes sweat with a white handkerchief. *Don't stroke out on me, Wayne, boy. You have to get us back to the car.*

He says, "Sam, your family—great grandparents, grandma and grandpa—farmed this land with their bare hands and a team of mules. This is where your Aunt Cecilia and your Daddy were born and raised. Me, too."

He waves at the hills marching off toward St. Louis. Even Vietnam, I guess, if you keep going, "Your Daddy's buried on that ridge. Somewheres. I was drunk as Hogan's goat when I finished his grave. Started drinkin' when the letter came saying they were escortin' his body home."

He shakes his head. "Took off out of here 'fore the funeral. First time back in over 50 years." He tosses a rock into the air and swings a small stick at it.

"God, how your daddy loved baseball. Great hitter. Good shortstop. Pros were interested, but he joined the Marines. Cecilia said they buried his bat and glove with him."

Hear that, Sam? Is that where your love of softball comes from? Like father, like daughter.

I swallow the lump in my throat. I'm fifty-three years old. As a kid, I hungered to meet my Daddy, even learn his name. "Don't nag," Mom would say. "I told ya. Art Carr. A Marine. From Missouri. I think." She was never good at details.

"You didn't take even one carnival booth photo?"

She walks away, shaking her head.

I learned Arthur G. Carr's home town, his enlistment date, next of kin, the date he was killed from the Marine Corps. When I visit Mom in the Home, she says they have long conversations. "He loves his little girl." She squints. "Reminds me of you. 'Cept her hair is wavy brown, not mousey gray like yours."

* * *

San Francisco.1964. A handsome young Marine, off to war. A pretty girl, tasting life. Marijuana, by the kilo. Booze, by the bucketful. Two days of wild sex. He ships out with feeble, "I'll write you's," and other lies. Nine months later, a baby. Me. About the time he was killed.

Now, on a green Ozark hillside, Wayne says, "I'd look under that big oak if it was me."

Once an asshole, always an asshole.

I found Wayne's name and number in a St. Louis phone book late one night. Bastard girls with ditsy, single Moms make desperate phone calls. I called him three times in high school, visited his small, cigarette-smelling apartment my senior year.

When sober, it was always the same story. "Yes, Art Carr was my brother. Yes, he could be your daddy. No, he didn't marry your momma. But who cares? Wish I could help more. I ain't got a picture, or a pair of his socks to give you. He was killed in 'Nam. About did me in, too."

A phone call a year, then two months ago, he called. "I'm sober and goin' home to right the past. You're welcome to come along. Visit your Daddy's grave."

He should have said hike hills, wade rivers, swat mosquitoes and sweat, with no cell phone service or internet. Now, he admits he was too drunk to remember where he buried his own brother. *You're a dumb ass, Sam getting mixed up with his kind.*

Andy leads me to a tree, tall as a San Francisco high rise. My foot kicks metal. Andy sifts dirt and leaves, then hands me a piece of rusting tin. "Art Carr USMC 1939-1965 RIP."

I'm surprised. "My Daddy's grave?"

Wayne comes up, his hand warm on my shoulder. A tree with droopy green limbs grows from a grassy mound. Wayne touches it like it's gold. "A Weeping Willow, survives only if it gets lots of water. Yer Daddy's tears kept it watered."

He puts his hat over his heart. "Art, here's your daughter, Samantha. You'd be proud. A fine lady, tough as nails." He wipes his eyes. He looks at me. "See, Sam? Yer Daddy was expecting ya all along.. Satisfied now?"

I shake my head. I'm not that easy. For over half a century I yearned to know more about my Dad than his name and serial number. A piece of rusty tin and a tree growing from his grave won't take the hurt away. I'll cross a few more rivers. Then we'll see.

The End

AFTER MIDNIGHT

AFTER MIDNIGHT

Most onto five hours ago, we come up onto where Ryman will fight his bare-knuckle extravaganza. When he seen them red-white-and-blue banners bearin' his picture and nickname, "The Ozark Bull," hangin' everwhere, he says to nine-year-old, Winder, "See what they done for yo' Daddy?"

Ryman's gonna take home a pile of cash money when he whups the black champ's ass. St. Louis fight fans pile into the cattle barn, eatin' barbeque, fried chicken, hamburgers, fried okra and other goodies washed down with Griesedieck Brothers beer. All this moola flyin' 'round means Mr. Harland Besler, the top boss 'round here, is gonna slap a fat calf in the ass tonight.

I'm Dummy. Scarecrow to some. Ryman calls me Zee. Real name's Hamus Zanderhook. I mostly do what Ryman asks - sweep out blood and muck after he's knocked some young man with more money 'n brains into next week - and care for Ryman's three young daughters though I'm at a crossroads there since they need a woman's touch, which I can't give 'em.

When Ryman agreed to fight in St. Louis, I was taken‘cause money ain't his need. after a hard-three-day drive over rocky, muddy roads Lon Warfield stopped his pickup ‘fore a tall green fence that hides Besler's two-house spread from pryin' eyes. Ryman pushes a button, a bell rings and the white gate swings open. Besler's crew commences right then and there to treat us like we was Lucky Charles Lindbergh or somebody special, I tell you.

Mr. Harland Besler hisself, shakes hands all 'round and waves us into his parlor all fixed up with black leather chairs and blue-and-white divans. Winder's eyes go big as snowballs and he grips my thumb hard.

Besler says, "Welcome to my humble abode. I moved the ladies out to give you privacy. Want anything? Ask. It's yours. I've got a Zenith that brings in Denver and Chicago with no static." He points to a tall wood cased radio with gold dials. "There's dominoes, checkers, and cards in the chifforobe. Cook on duty, day and night. Fancy a young lady? Take your pick. My treat."

Lon Warfield smiles big at this, but 'fore he can say anything a colored gentleman in black vest, white shirt, and black britches bows us to our lodgin's. Each room has two beds with red-and-green covers. The carpet's pink and blue showin' a four-legged animal sportin' a man's head gallopin' in the woods. Fuzzy pink wallpaper shows bare-bosomed ladies hangin' round a waterhole, eatin' grapes and drinkin' from tall cups.

Down the hall is a room with a bathtub, a dressin' table with a silver mirror and bottles big and small filled with colored potions sittin' on shiny trays. Lon says it smells like a Chinese whorehouse on payday. It makes my head hurt.

* * *

Winder's my special charge at his daddy's slugfests, never more 'n a lantern shadow away. He holds my shirtsleeve while the clown on stilts wearin' Uncle Sam pants and stovepipe hat twists balloons into dogs and flowers and hearts. I nab a green poodle, 'fore a tiny fella, dressed in what Ryman calls a tuxedo, snatches the clown's hat and scampers up a ladder.

The little guy does didoes and handstands, even beds down in the hat, while the bumpkin, green curls floppin' reaches and lunges for him. Finally, the midget's nabbed. He squirms this way and that, 'til his shirt and britches come off. Sure nuff, he ain't a he, but a pretty red-headed she, wearin' only her birthday suit. She grabs a rope danglin' from the ceilin' and climbs onto the Griesedieck Brothers beer sign, wavin' and bowin' to her audience. She 'most falls off her high perch twice, then throws kisses to all and dives, purty as a fallin' star, into a glass horse trough filled with water on the ground below. Folks clap and whistle. They like this a lot, I tell ya.

I ought to've put my hands over Winder's eyes while this were goin' on but didn't. Inside the barn, healthy-lookin' young ladies in yellow shorts and black polka-dot tops sell four-bit beer to thirsty customers. Fight fans who paid a buckstand shoulder-to-shoulder clean back to the hay bales. A dollar bill buys a grandstand seat up front. Them with a fin to spare, sit in blue upholstered chairs mebbe ten feet from where the fighters come to scratch, smokin' cigars and sippin' whiskey cocktails.

To the rear, on hay bales piled to the rafters, sit the colored folks, men in round hats and white shirts, ladies in Sunday go-to-meetin' dresses and big hats. They gab and laugh. They paid fifty cents each for this honor. Yessiree, Bob, Mr. Harland Besler's got hisself a goin' Jessie, I tell you.

The stock pen where Ryman'll fight the black champ, Max Hereford, has been whitewashed, the slats replaced by ropes with fresh sawdust spread over the dirt. The square circle, Besler called it last night

.

* * *

"We promoted this as hillbilly against colored, since every defense plant and factory has plenty of both," Besler said last night, glancing' at Ryman. "No offense meant, nor taken, I hope. Folks skipped meals to see you beat that black boy's ass, Ryman. I'll be in the office, so I won't see it. Sure hope you knock him into la-la land."

We no more'n get settled in, when Lon Warfield asks Ryman if he feels the need to loosen up some. This throws me 'cause Ryman's trained hard for this scrap. He split logs and stacked firewood, pushed wheelbarrows filled with rocks up past the sassafras and persimmon trees and dumped 'em in the gully. He carried sacks of rocks and sand from the crick uphill to the barn and back. Breakfast and dinner, he ate spinach and scrambled eggs with tomatoes. For supper, liver and onions.

Lon and Ryman go outside and commence to play fight on the lawn between the two houses. They's pops and grunts roust out the ladies, and 'fore you can say, "Pretty girl, pretty girl," a dozen of 'em, in bed clothes, stand under the sugar maples, gigglin' like Sunday School girls. A perfumey smell fills the air.

A skinny blonde spies Winder. "Come here, boy, so I can see ya up close. Ain't been 'round a little one since I left home."

Me and Winder sidle over. Skinny pats Winder's shoulder. "I got one 'bout yer age. Somewheres." She plants a big kiss on his forehead. Winder's eyes go big as walnuts, his face firebrick red. 'Fore he can wail, I put a hand on his shoulder to let him know it's okay.

Skinny says to me, "Where'd ya get them scars? Stand too close to the fire at a weenie roast?"

"Keep it clean, Norma," says a older lady in a pink robe with white feathers down the front. "No weenie talk. 'Sides, you ain't seen one for a week." The other girls laugh.

Robe Lady says, "When I were a girl, our dog knocked over a lantern. Burned down the barn and set little brother on fire." She looks to the sky. "That boy had bad luck his whole life. Drowned dead the next summer."

Skinny says, "This one didn't drown, but he oughta. With his face." She points at my lower part. "Everthing work down there?" The other girls giggle like she's Gracie Allen on the radio.

Lon's tuckered out and throws up his hands. Ryman says, "Come here, son." Winder crawls on his Daddy's back and Ryman gives him a ride by doin' pushups.

The ladies like this. "Want me to get under ya?" And, "Whatja charge for that?"

Ryman says, "Behave. Or I'll spank ya."

Skinny says, "Start with me. Please."

After a few minutes Ryman motions me over with his concoction of chamomile tea, stewed mint, fine-ground walnuts, and boiled horsetail root. He drinks while I towel him off. Robe Lady says, "Show's over, girls. Back to work."

Lon eyes a redhead. "I like yer style."

"I like you too, Lover. Come visit. Ask for Clarisse."

Lon nods, starts to follow her, sees Besler and Ryman headin' inside. He runs to catch up. I busy myself by pickin' up towels. Blondie's near the rose bush. She whispers, "I were fun-nin' ya, Scar Face. Name's Norma. Like to entertain ya, okay?"

I shake no. Ladies of the night ain't to my likin'. I head inside. At the door, I look back. Skinny, hands jammed in her robe pockets, shoulders slumped, her face the color of oatmeal, squints toward the house, hopin' for one last glimpse of Winder, I reckon.

* * *

Besler scheduled two fights 'fore Ryman's match, what he calls the undercard. Ryman changes into fight gear and drowses on a cot, waitin' to be called for his fight. Lon, tall as a park statue, guards the door. He's Ryman's driver and covers bets for Ryman's fights. He keeps his pistol shoved in his waist band. Ryman says Lon can shoot and gut a deer 'fore its last turd hits the ground.

I take Winder outside to run off his piss and vinegar. He races here and there, slows to watch the dogs do tricks, rides the merry-go-round, and has a cotton candy. When the microphone blares that a fighter can't come to scratch, we hurry inside and follow Ryman to the square circle, me carryin' his ice bucket and and towels, Winder luggin' his Daddy's stool. Ryman wears the black and red robe Besler given him and raises his hands over his head as he walks.

* * *

This is Ryman's first bare-knuckle go 'round in a big city like St. Louis. Two months or so ago, Besler drove his Caddie to Mokane the Saturday night Ryman knocked out Boxcar Adams in the first round. Boxcar's twenty years younger and forty pounds heavier than Ryman, but he got carried out on the cellar door, his face bloody sausage, his jaw broke, belly swole up from Ryman's fists bangin' his kidneys.

After the fight, Ryman in clean overalls and blue shirt open at the collar, and Mr. Harland Besler, his gray snap-brim hat pushed back on his head, wearin' a brown suit coat with a white shirt and blue-and-yellow flowered tie and brown-and-white shoes, drink beer in the Blue Moon Cafe.

Besler says, "Fight for me in St. Louis and you'll eat coconut cake and beefsteak every day, with money left over to buy a new Farmall tractor."

Ryman smiles. "I'm a big fish in a small pond 'round here. I like it that way. With the real men off to war, I've been lucky to win a few fights and make a dollar or two. When the war ends, so does my fightin'." Ryman's good at poor mouthin' hisself.

Besler says, "When the war's over we all move on. But, you could have a couple of big paydays between now and then. Hell, the St. Louis Browns have a one-armed ball player playing outfield for them."

Ryman nods. Truth be told, he's knocked many a strappin' young man to his knees, beat some 'til they'll cripple through life, and taken home 'nuff fight pots to pay cash money for eighty acres of prime farm land 3 miles west of Yellowbird on Layer Creek, with a good house, outbuildin's and spring-fed crick. Ryman don't need money. What he needs, and I think he'd agree, is a good woman to help him raise his 3 girls and rein in Frankie, his 6-year old boy, and kinda guide Winder when I ain't 'round. You don't win wives at bare-knuckle jamborees, just one-night companions.

* * *

The announcer introduces Ryman as "The Bull of the Ozarks" and says he ain't never been whupped, nor knocked down. He calls out his name loud and long. Most white fighters won't take on a colored boy, but Ryman'll fight Paul Bunyan and Babe, his Blue Ox, at the same time if the money's right. I reckon tonight's pot must be sweet or Ryman wouldn't be here.

When the announcer calls the black champ's name, the boos and name-callin' start. "We don't shoot coloreds here; we bury 'em." And, "That black boy won't fight 'til he gets some watermelon." Other yells are plain nasty.

The gong rings for round one. Twenty minutes of hard knuckles tearin' skin, eye gouges, and fists to the gut. Max comes out like it's Christmas mornin' and he expects a fine present. He pops Ryman mebbe five straight punches. Ryman flicks 'em off like horseflies. To show he come to the party, Ryman fires right hooks and left jabs, but hits only air. I reckon that's why they call Max, "The Shadow."

The gong rings. Four rounds left. At his stool, Ryman says, "This boy's quick as a quail. If he could punch, he'd whup my ass."

Ain't it written in the Good Book to choose your words

with care, since you live by what you say?

* * *

Round two, Ryman's punches miss Max here to Wisconsin. His face is red and he's breathin' hard. Fed up with a fighter who won't stand still, Ryman grabs Max with a rasslin' hold and aims a fist at his chin. Max jerks back.

Ryman's punch slams into Max's Adam's apple. His eyes go big as biscuits. He gurgles like water pourin' from a jug. Ryman lands a hard left to Max's nose and a right to his chin. Blood and snot fly. Then, Ryman slaps Max with his open hand. The crowd roars.

They know this is Ryman's way of sayin' piss on the fire, the party's over, that he's gonna wreck this fella, mebbe put out a eye, and for sure, knock him into next month. That's what they come to see.

Max's legs are spread, his arms adangle. He seems confused as a man in a dress shop. Ryman slaps him agin, then fires a right upper cut. Max staggers. Ryman gives him the ole one-two. Max's knees buckle. He grabs onto Ryman to keep from eatin' saw dust.

Ryman yells, "Turn me loose, boy!"

Max keeps holdin' on. Ryman pushes him with both hands. Max figgers he's about to die, fires a overhand right. It lands smack on Ryman's chin and sends him sprawlin'. Max rubs his throat tryin' to breathe, with no idee his blow knocked Ryman down.

Next to me, Winder pulls at my sleeve. "Get up, Daddy. Get up!" Ryman lays still as a walnut log. "Get up or you lose."

Winder's right. If the gong sounds now, the fight's over and Max wins the pot, sendin' Ryman home with purple bruises and a bloody nose and no money to soothe the hurt. I want to run out and jerk Ryman to his feet but squeeze Winder's shoulder instead.

In the sawdust, Ryman crawls to the ropes and pulls hisself up. He wobbles like a dog with hydrophobia toward Max and pops him with a short right and good left. The gong rings.

When round three starts, Ryman slaps Max mebbe twenty times, while Max does his imitation of a fence post, standin' still. Ryman fires a hard right that splits Max's nose open. Blood spews five feet. The crowd is on they's feet, yellin' and hollerin' for Ryman to do Max in. Ryman says, "When I'm finished ever yer own momma won't know ya."

His punches look and sound hard, but true fight fans know Ryman's nursin' Max. He could knock him out now, but knows the crowd likes to see blood. After maybe 3 minutes, Ryman fires the old 1-2 to Max's gut. He crumbles like a saltine cracker. Ryman yells, "Get up, boy. Get up. I ain't finished with ya."

Max staggers to his feet, bent as a old man. Ryman slaps him agin and agin. Blood splatters on the rich fans in the blue seats. Ryman sends a left to Max's jaw, a right to his temple. Max falls like a shot hog. The sawdust he fell into turns dark. A smell like a over-turned privy fills the air. Ryman raises his hands over his head.

The timekeeper calls, "Fighter has to come to scratch."

Max stands, his knees wobbling,' then he falls. He struggles to his feet. His legs go weak and he falls face first into the saw dust. The timekeeper yells, "Black fighter quits. Fight's over." He hits the gong.

Ryman bows to his fans. They yell and shout. Some fans march and sing when the band plays "For He's a Jolly Good Fella." I towel sweat and blood from Ryman's chest and arms. Winder kisses his Daddy's cheek.

Ryman says, "C'mon." We cross over to Max's corner Mr. Timekeeper comes up. He kicks Max's foot. "Get your black ass up and out. Cattle comin'."

Ryman says, "Hey. Let him catch his breath."

Blood oozes from a cut over Max's eye, his lips are swole big as persimmons. He probably lost a tooth, mebbe two. I hand him a wet towel. He wipes sweat and blood from his face. His corner man looks at us like we have rattle snakes in our pockets.

Max's bullfrog voice croaks, "Mr. Ryman, ya rassled me."

"Part of the game, boy. Like holdin' when ya get knocked down."

The Timekeeper says,"Stop yer yappin.' Cattle's comin'."

Ryman says, "Show respect. He put up a good fight."

"Don't high-hat me, pal," the Timekeeper says. He pulls Ryman to one side. "Ya was on yer ass when time run out. If I hit the gong, he wins. Besler wouldn't want that."

"It was a lucky punch."

"Don't matter. Ya was down. I give ya extra time for ya to take this boy."

Ryman pulls his fist back to pop this liar a good one, but Lon Warfield shoves Ryman aside. "That's my job." He kept Mr. Timekeeper from a five-minute visit to the stars, layin' on his back.

Ryman taps Lon's shoulder, "Give him a twenty. But, I didn't need his help."

"Who said ya did?" Lon drops to one knee and pulls a wad of bills from his sock. He palms the timekeeper two tens. *Why didn't he take the gettus from the sack in his belt?*

Ryman motions at Max. "Feller has to feed his kids. Drop him a twenty."

Lon looks at Ryman a long minute, shakes his head, yanks out his wad and throws down a handful of singles.

"'Preciate it, Boss," Max says, spittin' blood.

* * *

Ryman pulls on Besler's gift robe with "Ozark Bull" wrote in green letters 'cross the back. We climb through the ropes and head outside. Lon calls, “Make way for the Champ.”

Everwhere folks yell Ryman’s name. “That black boy weren’t tough as he bragged.” And, “He’ll think twice ’fore he fights a white man agin.”

Outside, the crowd’s stacked up like logs in a beaver dam. Beer drinkers stand three deep at tables along one side, funnelin’ folks agin the cattle barn wall. Manure dust is thick as fog. Lon keeps sayin’, “Make way for the Champ.”

The clown on stilts lopes past, his arms flappin’ like a scarecrow in the wind, the girl midget ridin’ his back. She has on her clothes now, but folks whoop and holler just the same.

That’s when it happens.

* * *

With the crowd yellin’ at the clown, a man with a blue bandana coverin’ his face like a bandit in a Gene Autry movin’ picture show, jams a gun in Lon’s face. “I’ll take the money.” He jerks the sack from Lon’s waist.

At ‘most the same time, a second crook waves a pistol in my face and yanks Winder away from me. Some folks see the gun and surge forward to get away, knockin’ Lon to the ground. His gun hits the dirt and spins to a stop agin a table leg, mebbe three feet from me.

The robber’s eyes were on Ryman, ‘fraid he’ll grab Winder, so they didn’t see Lon’s gun fall. The feller holdin’ Winder says, “Don’t do nothin’ stupid, Old Man.” He taps Winder’s head with the gun barrel. “Stay back and we won’t shoot him,” he says.

My heart jumps. *Would he shoot Winder?*

The crook with the money sack says, “Mike’s bringin’ the car.” Then, his voice louder, “Keep back, folks. We jist want the money. Do as I say and nobody gets hurt. Once we’re outta here, we’ll turn the boy loose.”

That’s they’s plan, huh?

I see headlights comin' up the road, fast. Mike, I figger. The beer drinkers push agin me, on both sides, cranin' they's necks to see what's happenin'. I don't know why I do what I do, but usin' these folks as a shield, I drop to my knees, grab Lon's .38, and crawl like a rabbit under three, mebbe four tables. When I stand, I'm behind the bad guys. My hands sweatin', my mouth dry as a cottonwood leave, I pull the hammer back and point that ugly gun at the sonofabitch holdin' Winder.

Mr. Timekeeper, sees me. He yells, "Let the boy go!" He waves somethin' shiny in the air. "I'm the law. We got a gun at yer back." I learn later his day job is deputy sheriff.

A robber yells, "We ain't fallin' for that old trick."

The car I seen speedin' up the road skids to a stop, fifteen or twenty feet away. dust swirling, making it hard to see. *Mike's here.*

The thieves back toward the car. Winder spies me and lunges. The bad guy carryin' him stumbles. Lon's gun jumps. A loud bang hurts my ears. Blood spurts.The robber falls. Winder slams into me. I drop the gun. We fall in a heap. Blue smoke fills my nose.

Two ladies push through the crowd. One grabs Winder. "He's too young for this shit," she says. It's the pretty midget girl the clown got nekkid earlier.

* * *

Mike, in the car, musta figgered he was on his own. He swings the car in a circle and speeds for the stockyard gate. He rams into a cattle truck. His Chevy leaps into the night, then slams on its roof, wheels spinnin.' Wild-eyed cows jump from the truck and run into the crowd. The car horn blares. Truck lights gleam yellow.

Mike crawls from his car and runs toward the gate, sees a crowd has gathered, and dives into a culvert near the gate. It takes Lon mebbe ten minutes to pull him out and drag him to the deputy, who makes him kneel 'fore he ties him with rope. His criminal days are over.

When the other robber seen his buddy hit the dirt when Lon's gun went off, he threw up his hands and yelled, "I give, I give." Ryman coldcocked him to make that a true statement. Now, roped to his buddy, his eye swole black, his nose bloody, he mumbles through broke teeth, "Forgive me, Lord Jesus. Forgive me."

A hour or so later on, the hearse comes. Two men in white load the dead body in and the deputy ties his prisoners to the dead man's legs. Then, he takes out his note book and says to Ryman, "I'll write this up as boys at a sportin' event when criminals horned in. An unidentified spectator shot and killed one of 'em. In self-defense. Protecting private property. That's it. Still, you best get over the county line fast, so me and Besler have wiggle room in case a politician or some damn preacher comes meddlin'."

We stop at Besler's office for Ryman's pay. As we go inside, Lon says, "Them robbers was sure dumb. They grabbed a sack stuffed with newspaper. That clown on stilts brung up the real stuff." He laughs. "I put Ryman's bettin' proceeds in my sock."

Mr. Harland Besler don't seem bothered one whit by the night's happenin's. He waves us to a seat. "Great fight, Ryman You buggered that colored boy up good.That's what folks spend good money on tickets."

Ryman don't smile. "Glad to be of help. But, this excitement ain't fer me."

"I hear ya. But, it's part of the game. Some idiot thinks he's entitled to someone else's dough and uses a gun to get it." He slaps my arm and laughs. "But Ol' Dead-Eye Zee made him pay."

He ain't one-bit funny.

Besler says, "Ryman, when things simmer down, I'll

schedule you again. Bill you as state champ. Give you a belt or a crown before the fight maybe."

His diamond ring catches the light. He hands Ryman a stack of bills thick as a Bible. "Half cash, half bank draft, like you asked. Here's my breakout."

Besler points to numbers on a paper. "Check my arithmetic. If I give you too much, keep it. If I'm under, let me know. Twice your usual winnings, right?"

Ryman glances at the figures. "Much obliged." He stuffs bills and paper into his overall bib.

I reckon Ryman don't need to worry that Mr. Harland Besler made a mistake countin' his own money.

Besler tousles Winder's hair. "Come back next summer. We'll go see them Cardinals play." Ryman planned for us to take in a ball game this trip, but the shootin' changed that.

Besler rubs his first finger and thumb together. "I've some influence 'round here, but the deputy's right. Get across the county line. Quick." He shakes Ryman's hand agin and slaps my back.

"Hear you play the fire out of a banjo. Bring it next time. We'll put you onstage so folks can see the real Dead-Eye Dick." He's jokin' about where the bad guy got shot. That ain't funny neither.

Outside, Ryman asks Lon, "How'd the bettin' go?" Lon grins big and hands him cash money and a paper. "Not many bet agin ya."

"Good. Take your cut?"

"No, sir. It's all here 'cept them donations to the deputy and Blackie."

Ryman hands the wad back and says, "Take what I owe ya." He sticks Lon's paper in his overall bib. "Nice haul. But was it worth it? The shootin' and all." Lon don't answer.

In the truck, Ryman snaps his fingers. "Damn, I near forgot. Lon, ya need liver for yer pup, don't ya?" He scratches his head. "We can't go back to Besler's for that redhead ya took a likin' to. There a house in St. Charles?"

Lon shrugs. "I might could find one."

Ryman pulls out a ten spot. "What's the price of stink nowadays?"

Lon says, "I'll skip tonight and stop by my sister-in-law's at home. My brother don't mind and she kinda likes it."

This takes me aback. I know the hefty lady he speaks of. She buys blackberries and walnuts from me in season. Step on her lawn and she squawks like a schoolteacher. She feeds eight or ten cats twice a day in her backyard.

Ryman says, "Hell, go double. Get a little tonight. More later. Man can't get too much stink." He stuffs the ten in Lon's shirt pocket.

That's Ryman. He knows crackle makes people jump. He spreads his jack 'round, so they jump higher for him.

Lon fires up his truck. I pull the tarp 'round me and Winder. We're hardly on the road 'fore he commences to jabber. "Sombitch put his gun in my face. Smelled like cow shit. His teeth were rotted. Glad you shot his ass."

Usually when Winder blackguards, I tweak his ear and shake no. Now, I hold him close. I'd like to tell him he's safe, that it's all over, but a house fire burned away my talk box. The only sounds I make are tongue clucks and shushes.

I close my eyes and ask Jesus to remove this stain from my memory. Then, my hand jerks and a eye swims by black as a crawdad hole. All sleepiness leaves me. If I had my banjo, I'd play my hurts away.

* * *

'Fore I can say, "Good time, Saturday night," the truck rocks to a stop in front of a beer joint. Lon, eager for the wiles of a lady, drove fast. The clock in the jewelry store window next door reads twenty-two minutes after midnight. A red light shines from a second-floor window. Red Foley's "Tennessee Saturday Night" spills into the street from the tavern's music box.

Ryman says, "Lon, go take care of yer bidness. We'll be in the bar." Lon walks up a wood sidewalk to the buildin' with the red light. A man steps from the shadows. Lon hands him somethin'. A yellow light cuts the darkness. Lon disappears.

The whole time Winder's laid on me. He goes limp as a wet leaf, then jerks, stiff as a schoolmarm's paddle the next. *Why didn't I bring my banjo?*

"C'mon," Ryman says. "Soda pop's waitin'."

I wave him away.

"Boy asleep?"

I flash a thumbs-up.

Ryman heads for the bar and is back in a jiffy, a red soda pop for me and Dr. Pepper for Winder. "Lon won't be long," he says, "then, we'll head home. We got a long ride." He slaps my shoulder.

"Ya done good tonight. I were a fool puttin' ya and the boy in that situation." He turns back to the beer joint.

I shake Winder awake. He sips Dr. Pepper. "My throat hurts." He sounds like he had sand for supper. He falls back on me, fast asleep.

If I had my banjo I'd pick a tune or two to make time pass faster. Still, I ain't no more 'n said the words to "Wabash Cannonball" and "Moonlight on the Pines" when Lon strides past, headin' for the bar. He's back in a hurry, carryin' more soda pop.

Most nights after a bare-knuckle slam bam, me and Winder sit on a bar stool and drink soda fizz while Ryman brags how he knocked the stuffin' out of some poor sucker. If the place has a band, I'll mebbe pick a few tunes and jig some for the crowd.

Now, Lon says, "Ryman's cornered a gal. It'll be a while." He slumps behind the steerin' wheel. Lon don't drink liquor.

Three men in white sailor outfits come from the shadows. gigglin' like boys at a swimmin' hole. "That black-haired gal had tits big as a Holstein."

"I see ya drink straight from the udder." They all laugh.

"Reminds me of a girl back home. Asked her how many guys she entertains a day. Said twenty-five or more Saturdays."

"What'd you expect? That ya were her one and only and she loves ya true?"

"I miss my folks," says the sailor who spoke of the girl back home. They've walked too far for me to hear more.

* * *

The hands on the jewelry store clock move slow as moss grows. Winder's about pushed me through the truck bed. I stand, stretch, and think through all four choruses of "The Great Speckled Bird," Roy Acuff's famous song.

Then I recall my guitar-playin' buddy, Farley Jenkins. *I'll go see him. Mebbe we'll put a band together and play honky-tonks and radio stations like old times. Give Nashville a go, mebbe.* Two minutes pass.

I repeat the words to "My Pretty Little Pink," The Music Freaks theme song. The whole band was made of by crippled folks. We played most everwhere in Jeff City and Cole County. Me and Blind Abe, the best piano player the world ever heard, would stay up all night playin' music. That's how I learned to pick like I do.

My rear end probably has root growin' from it, I've sat so long. Lightnin' flashes from 'cross the river. Winder trembles with each thunder boom. *We're in for a toad strangler. Wish I'd brung a sweater and my banjo.* The wind swirls dust and dirt down the street.

Then, glory be, Ryman comes out, a lady at his side. Up close, she ain't as young as most he cottons to. She wears a tight red skirt and white high heels.

"I sure like you," she says to Ryman. "Let's go get better acquainted."

"Not tonight, Honey," Ryman says. "We're runnin' from the law. I'll be back this way in a month or so. We'll catch up then." He digs into his overall pocket. "Here's a little somethin' for breakfast. Or whatever."

The lady don't look at her windfall, just stuffs it in her brassiere. A drunk staggers down the tavern steps. Jimmy Wakely's "I'm Sending You Red Roses" plays on the music box. Ryman slides in next to Lon. "Let's go."

Lon sits up. "Now? Storm's comin'."

Ryman says, "The lady's husband's off work real soon. I got one shiner. Don't need 'nother. 'Sides, you got what we come for, right?"

Lon starts the truck, and we're off to race the rain. The lady waves as we drive off.

* * *

Polio. Polio. Polio. Lon's wiper blades scream that terrible word with every slap. Winder hangs on to me like a snappin' turtle to a fish. Winder's my special buddy since his birth. When he were a little shaver, come mealtime, he'd stand on my bench, chubby hands on my shoulders. The first bite was his'n, the next mine, 'til our plate were clean as a spring rock. My ugly scars and burned away lips ain't no bother to him. He knows my hand gestures, tongue clucks, and hisses. His forehead and cheeks are hot to my to my touch.

I put Ryman's hand on Winder's belly. "Shit fire and save matches, fuck a duck and see what hatches. He's got a fever. Think its polio?"

These days, when a young'un's face goes red from playin' Ante Over or he's pooped from Indian rasslin', or don't take a second helpin' of peach cobbler at the school picnic, folks fear its polio. Ryman included, I reckon.

At a church supper one Sunday 3 years ago, me and Joshua, the preacher's kid, played music and clogged for the folks. Afterwards, we was drinking sweet tea on the well when Josh stood up, laughed, twisted in a circle, and fell face down in the grass. Died two days later. Polio. That's why Ryman's worried.

"We need a doctor. Fast," he says to Lon.

* * *

Ryman wipes the windshield with a rag, the rain ghost white in our headlights.The wind lifts the truck. Lon tries to steer down the black tar stripe in the middle of the pavement.

"Wentzville the next town?"

"Yeah," Lon says.

"They got a doctor?"

"Beats me."

"See a light, stop."

Winder's legs are on me, his back on his daddy. The only sound is tires splashin'water and Winder's heavy breathin'. We drive. After a while we see a light. Lon pulls into a parkin' lot.

"Bring him," Ryman says. We're at a Walgreens. A sign in the window reads "Closed." Ryman shakes the door. "Open up. Need a doctor."

Cuss words come from inside. "I got a shotgun pointed at yer belly. Can't ya read? Store's closed."

"Put down yer gun, friend. There a doctor around?"

The night watchman's light plays on Ryman's face. His black eye, courtesy of Max Hereford, makes him ugly as Boris Karloff.

"Sawbones won't help you. Beefsteak'll take the swellin' down."

"Ain't me who needs doctorin'. It's my boy. Got bucked off a horse."

Ryman's smart to say this. If he said it might be polio, the watchman would run like a scalded dog and warn everbody to stay away. Polio scares folks that bad.

"Doc Hill would see ya. If he's sober. If he ain't, yer best bet's St. Charles. Doc's the corner house two blocks south. Big elm in the yard."

"Much obliged," Ryman says. "Bring me a jug."

"Can't. We're closed."

'Who says?"

Ryman lays a bill on the window so the watchman can see it. It's probably the first double ten he's seen in a while. Mebbe ever.

"'Round back. Side window. Ya didn't get it from me."

"I ain't never been to this fair city."

I carry Winder to the pickup and wait with Lon. Ryman's hat drips rain when he climbs in, carryin' a bottle. Lon drives slow. We see the sign. "Doctor's Office."

There's a light toward the back. Winder's heavy as wet hay. I flop on the porch swing. Ryman bangs the door. It opens a crack.

"Quiet. You'll wake the devil."

"Ain't him we're after. Need a doctor. You him?"

"Yeah."

His light plays on Ryman's face. "Can't help you. The swelling will go down in a week or so. You'll be fine."

"Ain't me. It's my boy. Has a bad fever."

"How long?"

"Hour. Mebbe longer."

"Can he move his arms? Walk?"

I lower Winder to the floor. He walks to his daddy.

Doc says, "If he's not paralyzed yet, it's probably not polio. Give him some aspirin powder. Put him to bed. It's after midnight."

"Wish you'd look him over," Ryman says. He holds the

bourbon so the light hits it. "Don't want this to spoil."

"That's a fact." Locks click. Chains rattle. The door opens. Inside, the office smells of rubbin' alcohol and sick folks. A sign on his desk reads, "H. Chase Hill, Doctor of Osteopathy." Framed letters and pictures are on the wall.

Doctor Hill twists the top off the bourbon and takes a long pull, swallows, takes 'nother nip, and says, "How old are you, boy?"

"'Most ten."

"You're small for your age."

"I can run faster 'n anybody in school."

"I bet you can."

Doc puts a thermometer in Winder's mouth and shines a light in his ear, then holds his listenin' device to his chest. I seen a doctor do the same to Blind Abe in Jeff City, once.

"Hurt anywhere?" Doc asks.

"Nope."

"That calls for a drink." He lifts the bottle and swigs. "Oh, yeah. No matter what, bourbon takes away the problem so it can grow bigger and hit harder later."

He pushes Winder's stomach. "Hurt?"

"I don't like guns in my face is all."

"I hate that, too." Doc turns to Ryman. "What's he talking about?"

"After tonight's fight, robbers used guns to try and steal the pot and kidnap him." He taps my shoulder. Hamas shot the main sombitch."

Doc eyes me. "You don't look like a killer."

"He don't talk," Ryman says. "But, he's a mean sucker when it comes to protecting his own.

I wish Ryman wouldn't josh so. I ain't family. Just a boarder.

Doc looks at Ryman. "Get that eye tonight?"

"Yeah."

"Win any money?"

"Some."

"Little old for that game, aren't you?"

"Figured I'd make a buck or two while the real men are at war."

"It's your blood. Your skin. Here's some APCs for the boy." He hands Ryman a small flat tin. "Win enough to justify putting your family in danger?"

"Hell, sweat dries. Blood clots. Bones mend."

"Smart ass, huh?"

Ryman's voice is strong. "No. Just some of us have to use what we've got to make it in this world."

"No offense meant," Doc says. "Here's something to chew on. One Fourth of July I left my family in the park and went to the beer garden. Came out three hours later to a dead daughter. Fireworks spooked a team of horses. They dragged her a hundred feet. She'd have lived if I'd been there to staunch the blood. I traded my daughter for beer."

He chugs the bourbon. "You're making the same gamble. Your boy sees and hears things he shouldn't at his age. With his protector—you—in danger, he gets upset and runs a fever. When he's older, he'll drive too fast, or stick a knife in someone's gut because he thinks he's pleasing you."

Ryman don't answer.

Doc takes another jolt of bourbon. The bottle's 'bout empty now. "Eat supper?"

"No."

"Skyline's open twenty-four hours a day. At the junction."

Doc's hand is on my shoulder. "You in a fire? That why you can't talk?"

I nod.

Ryman says, "Found him in the woods. Wet and cold. Near dead. House fire killed his Pap and little sister. My wife nursed him a year or more. Been with me since. Like family. She died two year ago."

Doc Hill nods. "Being wet probably helped his burns, if he didn't catch pneumonia. The way his scars run if he'd have talked, his larynx wouldn't have atrophied. Today, we'd hook him to a nebulizer and make him speak. Even sing."

He finishes the bourbon. "Why's everyone so wet?"

"Boys were in the back when the rain hit."

"A piece of advice. Treat folks better, they'll do more for you." Doc's voice is low. "My only loyalty's been to booze. All that's gotten me is puking drunks and hurt feelings. Most folks just want a kind word now and then."

He opens his desk drawer and moves things around. "Tried that stop drinking program a doctor in Ohio started. Not for me. Too many absolutes."

He hands Ryman a silver tube. "Calendula. For your eye. Reduces swelling. That'll be ten dollars. Plus the bourbon. Night calls are usually fifteen."

Ryman forks over a Jackson. Doc looks in his desk, goes behind the counter, opens a drawer, then stuffs the bill in his shirt pocket.

"Let me guess," Ryman says. "No change."

"Not tonight." Dr. Hill opens the door. "Drive slow. It's raining."

* * *

The Skyline is a Frank Sinatra kinda place. "Be Careful, It's My Heart" plays on the jukebox. In the men's room, I comb Winder's hair and dry his feet and shoulders.

When the Soup Jockey comes for our order, Ryman looks at her the way he does when he's washed up for supper after a hard day in the field and a cool breeze blows from the spring and the table's set with fried chicken and all the trimmin's.

"Look at the hide on that hare," he says. "My goodness

gracious."

The Soup Jockey smiles like she's known us for years. She has black eyes and black hair. "Where'd you get that shiner?"

"Prize fight. At the stock yards."

"For Harland Besler?"

"How'd you know?"

"He asked me to sell beer when he came through a couple weeks ago."

"Didn't see ya there."

"Wasn't. His girls do more 'n sell beer. If you get my drift."

Ryman smiles. "I do."

"You the hillbilly champ he bragged about?"

"Guilty."

"You look like a prosperous farmer to me, not a country bumpkin."

She writes our orders in a book. When I was Grill Master at the Upstairs Café in Jeff City, the waitress called in the customer's wants. "Noah's Boy" for a ham sandwich or "Take It Through the Garden and Pin a Rose on It," for hamburger with lettuce, tomato and onion.

Ryman watches the soup jockey go to the order window, then looks at Winder. He wipes his eye and clears his throat. "Doc had a point. I'd die if somethin' happened to him." His face works, his eyes shine.

His voice husky, he says, "I ain't done right by ya, Zee. Took ya from yer music, 'cause I needed help raisin' my kids. Not yer bidness. Ya give more 'n ya get."

He touches my arm. "Ever think 'bout goin' back? To the music, I mean?"

He keeps talkin'. "Since Ethel died, I've been a real asshole. To my own family, even. Don't know any other way, I reckon."

Miss Soup Jockey comes up. She has a raw cube steak

on a dish, a towel over her arm. "Mind if I put this on your eye? It'll reduce the swelling."

'Fore Ryman answers, she has the towel 'round his head, holdin' the steak agin his eye. He looks like he's from "Terry and the Pirates" comic strip.

Ryman touches her hand. "Right nice of you, Miss. I've got three girls at home. Thanks to Zee, they cook a little. Sew some. But with 'em gettin' older, he can't answer girl questions. Me, neither."

She smiles. "Girl's needs are different from boy's."

Ryman says, "Tonight's fight showed me I'm washed up. Couldn't hit that darkie with a shotgun. Had to put a rasslin' hold on him."

He waves a hand in the air. For the first time, I see the black bruises, fingers crooked as oak root. He tries to laugh. "That was the last time I fling fists fer money."

The Soup Jockey says, "Mind if I sit? Name's Janet." Glenn Miller's Orchestra plays "That Old Black Magic" on the jukebox.

"Glad to meet ya, Janet." Ryman holds her hand after they shake.

Then, for the first time I ever heard, he speaks of hisself. "I'm Ryman Call. Bare-knuckle fighter. Retired. This is Zee. Banjo man. My boy Winder is on his lap. I've a good house. Eighty acres of prime grazin' land. Plenty of water. Three girls to raise." He touches his eye. "And one helluva shiner ya just fixed. Hope it's my last."

* * *

Me and Winder ride with Lon the next day. Ryman and Janet follow in the 1940 Studebaker Ryman bought with his St. Louis winnin's. They was married at Yellowbird Baptist a year later. Farley Jenkins' song, "Knockout Love," about their courtship opened doors in Nashville for me and him.

I came back for Winder's high school graduation most onto nine years later. Like I done for years I took a Greyhound from Nashville to Jeff City, a taxi to Yellowbird, and walked the last 3 miles to Ryman's. At supper the first night, with the family gathered 'round a table groanin' with food, I wrote on my paper, "Doc Hill sure gave good advice."

Ryman reads my note, then gazes at Janet like a cow at her calf. "Doc said stop at Skyline. A certain woman there put a beefsteak on my eye and feelin's in my heart."

The End

★★★★★

RULES OF DYING

RULES OF DYING

Every work day morning at 8 o'clock sharp, me and Juan and Marcus and Willard stand at attention with hands over our hearts while the National Anthem plays on the loud speaker at Fort Rosecrans Cemetery. The Resident Supervisor, Captain C. T. Wallace, in his Navy Reserve uniform, runs the flag up, ties off the rope, salutes, and goes into his office.

I'm Mike. I ride herd on the crew renovating grave sites here at this place of rest for American vets. It ain't easy work. I speak un poco Espanola, and my crew is mostly Mexicans. My rule is when they conversate with each other they can talk Swahili for all I care, but they have to speak English to me. With this bunch, one minute I'm a mean ass drill instructor, the next a smiling priest

After the Anthem we watch a gray Kia Rio drive past. The driver, a young blonde wearing a blue pants suit, low-heeled black shoes and a white blouse, opens the car's trunk, grabs a green and white folding chair, yellow umbrella, and a white flower and carries these like birthday presents to her usual spot.

She sets up her chair, opens the umbrella to block the sun, and goes to the columbarium, where ashes of cremated bodies are kept. She unlocks a niche door, takes out an urn, about the size of a half-gallon of milk - the remains of the person she's here to mourn - holds it a minute, puts it back, stretches tall, removes yesterday's white geranium from its holder, and puts in today's flower then walks to her chair and sits.

Often, on the blue San Diego bay below us, like an art gallery painting, a submarine or aircraft carrier glides out to sea, past the Point Loma light house, with sea gulls circling and the sun turning the ocean silver and gold.

Once seated, the young blonde fits her i-Phone ear buds into small white ears, opens a thick book, wetting her finger with a pink tongue to turn the pages. She's still there at noon when we come up to eat lunch in the shade of the coral tree.

Juan says, "She's here ever day, for who? Husband? Brother?" He waves a tattooed hand in the air. "Every fuckin' day, rain or shine."

Willard asks, "How do ya know ever day? Ya work week ends?"

Juan says, "If the park's open, she's here. A husband, I bet. Not likely her daddy. She needs a man. Like me."

Juan's on probation. He got out of Donovan State Pen last January. He's edgy as hell standing at attention when the *Star-spangled Banner* plays but he does as told, gets to work on time and holds up his end when it comes to work.

Marcus asks, "Think she plays music on her phone?" Marcus and Juan are kin.

They ride to work together in Marcus' Bronco.

Willard says, "Classy girl like her? Probably religious shit." He's a tall drink of water. From New Orleans. Has more 'tats than an NBA player. Never done hard time, according to his application.

Marcus says, “Classy? You mean assy? She wants something hard. *Carne dulce.* I’m her man.”

I don’t say anything. These guys have different opinions about women than I do.

* * *

One noon, we’ve finished our tortas when Marcus grabs the weed whacker we use to barber the grass around a marker. He lopes across the road and begins to edge the sidewalk next to the girl’s chair. *What the hell!*

I run up. The blonde’s brown eyes go big. “Pardon us, ma’am. My man’s trimming grass that maintenance missed.”

“Yeah,” Marcus says, “Make it perfect for you.”
His hot, black eyes scorch her from chest to rear end. She’s wearing jeans and red tennis shoes.

Her voice is sweet as a phoebe’s call. “How nice.”

* * *

Back at the truck, me and Marcus have a go. “Dude. What the hell?”

“Wanted her to see a real man.”

A stupid thing, Asshole.”

“Oh, yeah? She liked it.”

“Really? Scared the shit out of her. Pull that trick again, I’ll write you up.”

“Yeah?”

“Yeah. Count on it.”

“Un hombre tiene que hacer lo que unhombre tiene que hacer?”

“Not on my watch, hombre.”

* * *

At 2 o’clock sharp every day, the girl stows her gear and drives off without aword. A young blonde driving a gray Kia slow as a funeral hearse.

* * *

Soil contracts at night and expands by day. Tree roots attack caskets. Gophers and rats dig tunnels. Rain and irrigation water wash away dirt so that head stones tilt or fall over. Sometimes, a casket splits open. Inside is rags and brass buttons, bones grey as gun powder, some no longer than a chicken leg.

Often we renovate a whole section, spreading caskets and markers name side up on the grass. Cemetery visitors swarm like yellow jackets, push past our yellow tape, taking selfies next to the caskets, interrupting our work, kicking clods into the trench and peppering me with questions. "What's going on?"

I answer, "Every hero deserves a beautiful and peaceful resting place, so we're doing repair work."

"There a body in every casket?"

"Absolutely. We're careful to see each grave is correctly marked."

That's a lie. Some stones mark where a body used to be, but caskets disintegrate and flesh rots. When we restore an area, we dig the markers out by hand before the back-hoe rips a trench. We lower a metal box into the hole and pour in reinforced concrete. When this starts to set, we replace the head stones, a man on each side, careful as moving a crate of eggs, tamp sand and pea gravel around the marker and replant the sod. That hummer will stand straight and proud as a soldier for years.

It takes sweat and know-how to cut away grass roots with a sharp shooter and pry out tree roots with a rough-neck bar or square up a trench with a spade, but it gives you time to think.

Eight years ago, as part of my rehab, the VA sent me to culinary school. I had my kids then. The restaurant job I got when I graduated wouldn't buy food, much less clothes for two growing boys and a young lady, so I hired on here. Now, me and the kids momma share custody two weeks a month. I make $12.38 *an hour, $18.56 overtime, with an extra twenty-five a week as a crew supervisor. I try to save a little each pay day so I can open a restaurant someday. Weekends only, with reservations-only seating.*

Saturday night, Cinda's coming for dinner. If she can find a sitter. She lives in that double-wide across the street and two trailers down at Clariton Estates Mobile Home Park. She has black hair and black eyes. When she smiles, her white teeth show, making my throat so tight I can't talk.

I'll start with an amuse bouche, say a celery-infused beef puree. For the primo, Bibb lettuce and endive, with a little arugula and radicchio for bitterness, tossed with quinoa and mushrooms, topped off with honey-roasted walnuts and organic plum tomatoes and a nice lemon garlic dressing.

What secondo will she want? Fish or chicken? I'll drop by her trailer tonight after her kids are down, say 8:30 or so, and ask. If fish, it'll be sea bass grilled in lemon butter and almond paste. If chicken, I'll wrap it in foil and smother it under charcoal with parsley, onions and green peppers.

The dulce? Double chocolate cake. I'll bake it Friday, after work.

While I work I think about cooking mostly, but sometimes my thoughts wander to the blonde in the beach chair by the columbarium. *Who's she thinking about?*

* * *

Willard and Marcus are having a lover's spat. They're kinda a team, I guess. If Marcus made a sharp turn, Willard would break his nose.

"What 'ya mean, rules for dying? Silliest thing I ever heard." He tosses the shovel away and picks up a hoe.

Marcus says, "There's five of 'em, man. When my nephew was offed, the social worker told us about 'em."

Willard makes a face. *"Tonterias!"*

"No bullshit. She named 'em." Marcus turns to me. "Tell him, Boss."

"You mean the stages of grief? Denial, anger, bargaining, depression, and acceptance?" I learned these when my sponsor's Dad died last year. He made a big deal out of 'em.

"Yeah. That's it."

Willard says, "When my Old Man took out that eucalyptus with his motorcycle, we knew he was dead. No denying it. Tore 'cycle and him all to shit." His face is red, and not just from work.

I nod. "Ever play over and over in your head how you could have kept it from happening? Feel sad at times? Think about it from time-to-time?"

"Everday. Normal, right?"

"Marcus' point is our mind goes though different stages when someone close to us dies. Thinking how you could have changed things is bargaining. Feeling shitty. That's depression."

Willard slices a lizard in half with his shovel. "I don't drive that street no more."

"Ain't that the shits?" He shakes his head.

Juan says, "What *staget,* how you say, stage, is our Little Darlin' goin' through?"

"Beats me."

"Is there a dickin' stage? That's what she needs. A good *jugando."*

* * *

A week or so later we're waiting for the back-hoe to make a trench. Marcus says, "Boss, I dropped my gloves at lunch. I'll go get 'em."

"Like hell you will. The other crew sees you, they'll say you're loafing and I'll have paper work for weeks. I make the big bucks. I'll go."

Marcus clinches and un-clinches his fist.

I ignore this. "Double check our measurements before

the back-hoe starts, okay? I'll be right back."

We eat lunch across from the columbarium because the benches there are in the shade, the rest rooms clean and close by. I go to where Marcus sat. No gloves. Trash can negative as well. I stoop to look under the bench.

A girl's voice interrupts. "Looking for these?"

It's the blonde from the columbarium, but she's not blonde any more. Now, her hair is pink and blue. She wears a yellow blouse, tight white jeans with holes at the knees and open-toe, sparkly sandals. Her Oakley sun glasses are silver-tinted. She hands me Marcus' gloves.

"That wild-eyed guy who trimmed grass around me last week dropped 'em. I was taking 'em to Lost and Found. You're the boss, right?"

I nod. "Thanks."

The small gold necklace around her throat says Misty.

"Misty, you're here every day. You read a lot. Fiction or nonfiction?"

She holds up a book. "Stuff Tate liked. This is *Do Androids Dream of Electric Sheep.*" She smiles. "I finished Harry Potter. The whole series." She holds up her phone. "I'm getting damn good at Grand Theft Auto, too."

"I'm impressed. Tate your husband?"

Her face pales. "Yeah. Army. Killed in Afghanistan. IED. Never saw his body. We were married one year, eight months and four days. At his memorial service I vowed I'd visit him 609 days straight."

She smiles. "Seventy-three more to go. You familiar with the Five Stages of Grief?"

"A little."

Her small white hand removes sun glasses. Big brown eyes. "I'm past denial but not anger. If I had a chance, I'd kill every fucking politician in D.C." Her eyes go black with tears. "My support group says we never fully recover, just survive."

She pulls a paper from her jeans "My work schedule. I waitress at a bowling alley café. Makes the time pass. Surviving. I can't date, though Tate says it's okay."

She blushes. "Isn't that crazy? I talk to my dead husband. And he answers." She puts her finger to her red lips. "Quiet, Misty. Tate says silence is sacred here." She smiles. "You agree?'

I nod.

She turns and walks to her chair, without a backward glance. A young girl with pink and blue hair, a small gold necklace with her name on it and holes in her jeans.

* * *

I'm Navy myself. The only one in my crew who served, but my bunch turns over so often, next week we might have four vets. I was stationed at Subic Bay in the Philippines for 2 years. Me and this LBFM did the khaki sack thing. Fell in love with the sex. That was a trip since I was into Jesus then. Back Stateside, I felt guilty. And horney. My pastor told me I could send for her. I did. We got married. She was religious. I was messed up over the sex. Booze and nose candy became my Gods.

Four years later, what a scene: Two squalling kids running the house, Baby Ruth preaching Jesus to me, and me swearing I'd taken my last drink. Wrecked my truck one night. Spent 42 days in the VA hospital in La Jolla. When I got out, I joined AA. Took me three years to get straight. Got fired as a heavy equipment mechanic. Took up small engine repairs, but the drugs made my hands shaky. Couldn't handle detail work. The VA said they'd send me to culinary school. A 3-month course. My kids are 16 and 17 now.

Last June, my daughter, Margaret, ran off. I found her at a shelter in Santa Monica over Thanksgiving. Needle tracks up both arms, her nose dripping snot. My heart bleeding in my chest. Like father like daughter, I guess

I visit AA rooms most weekends. Last night, the speaker

talked about the 3rd Step, where you make a decision to turn your will and your life over to God. Years ago, I told my sponsor I'd like to do that. He asked, "If two bull frogs sit on a lily pad and one of them decides to jump, how many bull frogs are still on the lily pad?"

"One," I answered.

"No, dummy. Two. Decidin' to jump ain't the same as jumpin'."

So, I jumped. Did all the fuckin' steps. The whole nine yards. That's why I'm sober today.

* * *

Getting ready for Cinda tonight, I clean the kitchen, wash my DAV china, shine both settings of silverware, spread a red and yellow beach towel on the table and put Martinelli's in the frig. I'll buy a cake since I didn't bake last night. I clean the bath room and change bed sheets. Mrs. Chase from the single-wide next door, I call her Mrs. Scuttlebutt, bangs on my door.

"Isn't it romantic? Cinda's husband brought her the sweetest bouquet. Spend the night. He wants them to try and make a go of their marriage again."

Damn. Damn and double damn. I guess it'll be chicken for lunch this week.

* * *

Sunday morning. I'm empty. *Does Misty visit her husband weekends?* I slam a Nine Inch Nails CD into my truck's player, grab some 5-Hour Energy and somehow end up at Ft. Rosecrans. Why I don't know.

What the fuck? Willard's Toyota is in the parking lot. I didn't expect this. He's walking toward Misty. I cross the grass to head him off.

He sees me. "Stay out of this, Boss!"

"Where ya goin'?"

He waves a pick handle at me. "Juan says she wants a

man. That's me."

I feel his body heat. He smells like a gut wagon from booze and sweat. His eyes are red.

"You can't just grab her."

"You didn't say shit when Marcus bragged what he'd do to her."

"No, but I should have. Think it through, man. Don't do something now ya can't undo later." Talking Program to a drunk is a waste of time, I know. Get 'em when they're sober. And shaky, the Big Book says.

Willard throws down the pick handle. He's breathing hard. Sweat glues his shirt to his back.

"I could take ya," he says, squaring up in front of me, fists doubled.

"I know you could." My breathe comes hard, too. I don't want to fight. "Walk away My Friend," I say, "and it ends right here."

He cocks his head. "Promise?"

"Promise. But don't come in Monday. HR will send what you're owed."

"Fuck." He doubles his fists again "I could still take ya."

"I know. Go to your car. Sleep it off."

He glares at me, takes a deep breath, turns and walks away. He sits for a while before starting his car and heading out.

* * *

It's early fall. I've got an almost new crew. After the Anthem we wait for the Kia to pass. It stops. Misty rolls down her window.

"Day 609," she says. "My last visit for a while. Thanks for your help."

"Thanks for your service," I come to attention and give her a hand salute. She laughs, waves and drives off.

Marcus is still with me from the old crew. At our work

site, he starts in. "Boss has a girlfriend. Ya sweet meat that little chick yet?"

"Cut the vulgar talk, man. Women like her deserve our respect." The guys look at me like I have two heads. "We've work to do. Let's go."

A black Toyota drives slowly by and parks. A man in a dark suit takes two chairs from the trunk and carries them to a grave with a tarp over it, then goes back to the car. He and a small lady wearing a black hijab walk toward the chairs, him holding her arm. They sit.

On the San Diego bay below us, sea gulls circle and the sun turns the ocean silver and gold, like an art gallery painting. An aircraft carrier glides past Point Loma Light House, going off to war.

The End

For more about Pete Peterson
and his stories:

Blog: https://petersonwriter.tumblr.com
Website: pete-peterson.squarespace.com

Made in the USA
Las Vegas, NV
08 August 2025

26064066R00125